REACHING THE UN-CHURCHED

REACHING THE UN-CHURCHED

PATHWAY TO CHURCH GROWTH

DR. MICHAEL W. WESLEY SR.

Townsend **Press**
Nashville, Tennessee

Printed and bound in the United States of America

24 23 22 21 20 19 18 17 16 15 – 10 9 8 7 6 5 4 3 2 1

ISBN: 978-1-939225-53-5

To the members of Greater Shiloh Missionary Baptist Church in Birmingham, Alabama, this research is affectionately dedicated. For more than twenty-eight years, this congregation has welcomed me and my family into their hearts, been patient while I learned to lead them, and given their support every step of the way. I thank my wife, Venita, and the office staff for many valuable contributions, support, and assistance during this process: Terri Daniels, Sheila Davis, Kristy Rather-Hall, Shirley Davis, and Russ McClinton.

I also dedicate this study to my beloved mother, who is in heaven today, Katye R. Wesley, who so inspired me to pursue every dream I ever dared to dream. She strongly encouraged me to earn a doctorate degree and to fulfill God's ministry plan for this church.

ENDORSEMENTS

Reaching the Un-churched is more than a how-to book or a blueprint. It is a book of dreams, visions, blessings, travesties, and courage. Above all, it is about one church with unfathomable faith in a God who always shows up at Greater Shiloh Missionary Baptist Church in Birmingham, Alabama. It is a story of a church where people recognize that the faithful hand of God is upon them. Dr. Michael Wesley is a gifted leader, pastor, writer, and family man. It has been my distinct honor to partner with this great church, and work alongside this godly pastor, who today I call friend. Before you read *Reaching the Un-churched*, prepare yourself. Get ready to shout, to cry, to dance, and to shout Hallelujah!

Bob Farris,
President
The Relevant Group, Atlanta, Georgia

Four years ago while working on a joint community revitalization project, I was introduced to a pastor of a church located in the west end neighborhood of Birmingham. I thought of this as an ordinary introduction; however, it proved to be different. It occurred to me that I had heard of him and some of the things he was trying to accomplish through his church's mission and vision. A member of his church had been a student in a couple of college courses I had taught in a local Bible college. This student had talked profusely about her pastor's skills as a preacher and teacher, and also spoke of the vision that he was trying to implement through the church and within the community. I promised that I would visit the church, but the opportunity to do so was slow in presenting itself.

Eventually, a personal introduction was facilitated through a mutual friend, as Dr. Wesley was on his way to another meeting. Despite the brief encounter, a definite connection was made. He related the synopsis of his vision for the church, and the kind of people that would be needed to see it actualized. A key element that raised my interest in wanting to hear more from him was the passion with which he communicated his vision and his goals. A few weeks later, my wife and I found time to visit the church, and after a couple of months, we united fellowship with Greater Shiloh. This preacher, teacher, and educator was not interested in maintaining the status quo; rather, he was seeking to implement important methods that would allow the church to become a change agent for the good of the church, its members, and the surrounding community. For four years now, I have been an eyewitness to the significant changes that our God has brought about through this pastor's visionary leadership. This journey is now documented in this new book, *Reaching the Un-churched*, which gives an insightful look into the systems that are demanded to be in place when change is required. These systems are supported both biblically and organizationally. Every student, teacher, pastor, and ministry worker should read this book and be challenged to understand that the Scriptures often speak about mission and vision. Seldom does one get to witness firsthand God filling in the specifics, which are interspersed in bringing the mission and vision of a specific organization to its targeted fruition.

Dr. Wesley has provided an accomplished, documented account of the work of the Holy Spirit, being used mightily to effect God's kingdom in an unlikely community. I am convinced that when these principles are adopted, they will send residual responses through many churches and communities throughout the country. Rarely is one given the opportunity to personally follow the impact created by the tentacles of change, but it is done for us in *Reaching the Un-churched*.

Rev. Frank E. Stone Jr.,
Assoc. Minister/Discipleship Director
Greater Shiloh Missionary Baptist Church
Adjunct Professor, Southeastern Bible College, Birmingham, Alabama

As a young pastor walking down a similar trail that Dr. Michael Wesley blazed several years ago, I must admit that *Reaching the Un-churched* has been an instrumental tool in my ministry. I am the fourth pastor of New Rising Star Baptist Church in the Eastlake community of Birmingham. My grandfather, Dr. Tommy Chappell, was the third pastor with the longest tenure of thirty-five years, serving as pastor from 1975 to 2010. *When God Changes a Church* has helped our church transition well.

Dr. Wesley tells of Greater Shiloh's journey as he transitioned from predecessor to successor. This is a recommended read for any pastor, especially those who are in transition. Change is physical, but transition is mental. Even after a physical change in pastoral leadership, it often takes more than a few years for the mindset of a church to catch up to the change that has already taken place. This book is for any pastor who has ever wondered, How do I build the future without tearing up the past? It is for any pastor who has ever questioned, How do I reach out to the world while reaching in to take care of the current congregation at the same time? How do I communicate the differences of the past without making the past seem deficient?

Reaching the Un-churched is a mentoring tool for every pastor. Mentorship accelerates time. What should take years is often able to happen sooner when people have mentors from whom they can glean. This book is filled with personal experiences from the heart, mind, and soul of Dr. Michael Wesley, as well as helpful research data and statistics. It gives hope to every pastor that dry bones in the valley can live again. It shows how God can change a church from just surviving, to striving for the future, to thriving.

Lastly, this book is a major investment in the future of the local church. One of the major values of this book lies in the reality that it gives the experience of an associate minister, who became senior pastor of the church where he served. Wesley's experience gives dual perspectives: the associate minister and the senior pastor. Many associate ministers learn to be great preachers and orators of the Gospel but have no biblical model to follow for leading a church. This book adds value for leading a church. It blesses associate ministers by granting them valuable insights on church leadership prior to being lead pastors and senior pastors, by granting direction for those who may need to turn around, and confirmation for those who are on the right path.

Dr. Thomas Beavers
Pastor, New Rising Star Baptist Church
Birmingham, Alabama

CONTENTS

PREFACE

When God Changes a Church!

When God changes a church, it transitions to become a church for the un-churched.

Greater Shiloh Missionary Baptist Church is a church with a rich historic past. It has maintained a presence within the community of Birmingham, Alabama, for 123 years. The past twenty-nine years has seen the church move through several distinctive periods. The eighties were a decade of decline, when the church's public presence almost disappeared from the radar screen. The nineties was a period of maintenance, and gave hints of renewal. The first decade of the new century the church was transitioning away from being an inwardly focused, traditional Baptist church, which had lost its evangelistic and missionary zeal. Well now into this second decade of the new century, the church has become an outwardly focused church, with an increased evangelistic heart for people who are marginally churched, and those who are un-churched. Greater Shiloh Missionary Baptist Church is now poised to reach people both locally and globally. We have become a megachurch that desires to be known more for its sending power than its seating capacity.

The genesis of this book was as a doctoral dissertation, completed for requirements at Louisiana Baptist University and Theological Seminary in 2006. The first edition of this book, published in 2010, chronicled the gradual but major intervention, designed to shift the thinking, understanding, and practices of Greater Shiloh Missionary Baptist Church. This second edition includes updates and offers greater clarity on the impact and progress of the research offered in the pages to follow. We trust that it will positively influence current and future leaders and laity alike.

The information contained here has already been proven and has propelled Greater Shiloh far out into a new future of community and global ministry. When applied, the principles discussed in this book, guided by the Holy Spirit, have the capacity to cause similar or even greater change in the life of most any church.

PART I

A Church in Need of a Change

George Barna, author of *Leaders on Leadership*, reports that over 80 percent of mainline churches in North America have either reached a plateau or are in decline. Greater Shiloh was clearly in a period of decline. Growth means change. The issue became how to inspire our congregation to embrace change. I understood the critical elements that would help our people embrace change: we had a crisis and we clearly saw the need to change, and we understood the full implications of deciding not to change.

Greater Shiloh needed a clear-cut, God-given vision. It is well known that a compelling vision can raise any church above mediocrity. Pastor and leadership guru Dale Galloway says that the leader's job is "to influence key people, and bring them together around God's vision." He further states, "That may be the most important thing you do as a pastor!" Cutting-edge churches have different styles and looks, but their senior pastors all share one characteristic—passion. Passion fuels vision, and vision drives mission. If a church develops a vision that is biblically centered, that church becomes outreach-focused.

The dominant ministry intervention selected to help Greater Shiloh rediscover God's vision and purpose for the church was the development of a strategic planning process; this provided guidelines and direction. It answered the questions about who we are, why we exist, and what we hope to achieve. Developing a strategic focus and process opened new paradigms that boosted the church's vision.

One such paradigm was embracing the value of incorporating an appropriate structure that anchored our new vision and organizing the ministries of the church into systems. We have been intentional to develop eight systems that not only clarify our vision but also categorize every function of a church. It has proven to be very effective. Examples in this resource will show how effective these systems have been. In our quest to discover what works today in cutting-edge churches, we have experimented with several minor ministry interventions that address different segments of our perceived concerns.

As a result of monitoring our annual strategic plan, one of the early minor interventions employed was Rick Warren's 40 Days of Purpose Spiritual Growth Campaign. We used that campaign to engage the entire congregation in a spiritual journey that led to a new level of missionary challenge. Another minor, but important intervention, was developing and implementing an annual leadership school, designed to define, develop, and deploy current and future church leaders with skills for various ministry opportunities. We learned that as we build leaders, they will build ministries; and as we build leaders, they will build churches.

In addition, we implemented a capital stewardship campaign, designed to unify the efforts of the community toward the construction of new facilities. The completion of that facility became a tool for new outwardly focused efforts. This capital campaign was a first for this church, and it carried members beyond the normal realm of thinking regarding church finance. During that first campaign, I did not preach on tithing; rather, I preached on vision and emphasized the need for the giver to give instead of the need for the church to receive. I wanted our people to know that giving is a spiritual discipline; if they neglect this powerful discipline, they neglect God, and choose to make money the master of their lives.

In June of 2005, the small congregation of 281 worshippers committed to give $1.3 million to fuel the vision cast during that capital campaign. The money was received over the subsequent three years. The process of that capital campaign mobilized and spiritually challenged the entire church membership. The result fueled a new momentum to finance the vision of mission for Greater Shiloh. Our mission statement, "to reach, teach, and baptize throughout the world, beginning in our community, fulfilling the Great Commission by the power and presence of the Holy Spirit until Jesus returns," took on new meaning.

Each of the previously mentioned interventions impacted different segments of the church population. They awakened both the necessity and urgency needed in the quest to change practices, and transition internally from a program-driven ministry to a purpose-driven ministry. The major goal was to cause Greater Shiloh to regain its evangelistic thrust. Today, we have moved from an inward, maintenance mindset, to become a church with a heart for people who are far removed from God. Our focus is to help believers become lifelong devoted followers of Jesus Christ.

Since the implementation and success of that initial campaign, our practice of utilizing cutting-edge ministry practices continues. One effort, developed by Nelson Searcy, pastor of Journey Church in New York, shows how systems in a church are like systems in the human body. This powerful discovery occurred when we evaluated our church practices and ministries. After careful analysis and evaluations we organized ministry functions into eight systems. It has become one of the keys to remaining healthy as a church. This process has enabled us to identify areas of concern. For example, when there is sickness in a part of our human body, we are declared ill; adjustments must be made and treatment sought to get that bodily system healthy and functioning again in order for the body to maintain health. It is also true with the church.

At Greater Shiloh, our systems are the following:

- Evangelism or outreach
- Discipleship or teaching
- Ministry or equipping
- Fellowship or caring
- Worship or weekend service
- Strategic planning
- Leadership
- Stewardship

Through the strategic system our overall focus remained consistent. The leadership system gave us a process for defining, developing, and deploying church leaders. As we implemented the stewardship system, which includes education, collecting, data input, banking, and all aspects of accounting, our congregation became more aware of and accountable for church resources.

Past practices revealed that we had been working in isolation in various functions, often duplicating tasks or overlapping responses. Communication was not always clear and territorial concerns flourished. These conditions contributed to Greater Shiloh's becoming more anemic. The adoption of a systemic approach produced clarity in each function and has resulted in a more informed congregation, harmony among team members, efficiency, and accountability—internally and externally. The bottom line revealed that church financials have steadily increased 12 percent annually.

Where It All Began

Today, in a community located in a southwest corner of Birmingham, Alabama, breathes the historic Greater Shiloh Missionary Baptist Church, the city's third-oldest African-American church. Shiloh Baptist Church, as it was originally named, was the marvel church of the city of Birmingham. Its founding pastor was the legendary T. W. Walker, who for the first thirteen years of his life acknowledged that he had been a slave, and was seventeen years old when he learned to read and write. Determined to make something of himself and his people, he began this fellowship on May 3, 1891, as a result of preaching supported by a society known as the Christian Relief Association. The little church grew to become one of the largest congregations in the city. Often, when the house was filled to capacity, a good part of the streets was filled with people who were anxious to get close enough to hear.

A very serious tragedy struck leaving an indelible mark on this historic fellowship. Robert H. Walker Jr. of Washington D.C. published the book *The Trumpet Blast* in 1902, which is a collection of interviews and recorded eyewitness accounts of the tragic event. Most of what is known concerning this event comes from Walker's book and newspaper accounts, which are located at www.bplonline.org, a website belonging to the Birmingham Public Library.

Walker reported that on Friday evening, September 19, 1902, the National Baptist Convention, an African-American organization, was holding its 22nd annual assembly at the Shiloh Baptist Church edifice, according to its agreement of 1901 in Cincinnati, Ohio. Two thousand delegates were present from several states. Professor Booker T. Washington, founder and President of Tuskegee Normal and Industrial Institute, of Tuskegee, Alabama, had accepted the invitation to address the convention on that night. In his recent biography of Washington, historian Robert J. Norrell called Booker T. Washington "the most famous and powerful black man in the United States." Thousands of people, who probably would not have left their homes that night, were out at Shiloh Church. Drawn by the natural trend of circumstances, without any particular motive, hundreds came to get a glimpse of the great man.

At that time, Shiloh was an impressive brick structure, and was located on the city's south side. It had been completed the year before, and was built to seat 3,000 people. Spectators, hoping to hear Washington, began arriving hours before the event, and all seats were taken well before the speaker arrived. People continued to push their way into the church, packing the aisles and stairways well beyond capacity. Washington was a captivating speaker, but it was a warm night, and with thousands of people inside, the room was sweltering.

When Washington finished his address, the massive gathering honored the speaker with tokens of respect. The crowd derived much pleasure from hearing him, and in response, the audience members who were seated stood to applaud. What happened next remains in dispute, but it is thought that Judge Ballou, a Baltimore attorney, raised from his chair a step behind the orator, and stepped forward to congratulate him. At the same time, a lady from the choir to whom the seat belonged occupied the delegate's seat. Not knowing that he had been deprived of his seat, Ballou stepped back to be seated, but to his surprise he was met with unpleasant remarks from another male, Will Hicks, a member of the Shiloh Church choir. Before any degree of understanding could be reached, harsh words were exchanged. Vindictiveness prevailed and, with excitement, drew cries from female eyewitnesses who exclaimed the word *fight* with great alarm. The sounds of the words were heard all over the auditorium, and were mistaken for the word *fire*. People in the crowded, noisy sanctuary took up the word *fire*, and nervously so, until people in the rear of the church started to scramble for the door.

The moderator of the convention urged, "There is no fire." The pastor of the church reiterated, "There is no fire," asking all to keep quiet. Panic gripped the audience, and there was a mad rush to exit the building. The stampede rose to a higher degree of pandemonium. The people, who had started out at the sound of fire, thought each entreating urge was a warning for them to flee for their lives. They mistook the word *quiet* for *fire*, and they mistook "there is no fire" for "there is fire."

The churning feet kicked up clouds of dust, and people in the crowd mistook the dust for smoke. The building had six exits, but many rushed to the main entrance. Hundreds were gathered outside of the church and on the front steps. Hearing the commotion on the inside, many people outside became curious and tried to work their way in, while those inside tried to work their way out. The first wave tumbled out of the front door and bodies piled on top of them.

As more people pushed from the main floor and down the stairs from the balcony, the crowd clogged the entrance like a cork in a bottle. Women fainted and others fell or were knocked down by those around them. In the entranceway, the bodies piled up 8 to 10 feet deep, and those on the bottom were trampled to death or suffocated from the weight. Within ten minutes, the panic was over. Dead bodies lay in the aisles of the church and the entranceway. Massive piles of human beings lay around the steps outside; between seventy and eighty people died at the church during the stampede. Hundreds more were injured, and within two days, the death toll rose to 104. The final toll was a record number of 120 people, trampled to death in that most tragic event. All the dead were African Americans. Most of the victims were residents of Birmingham, though the dead included people from Arkansas, Georgia, Kentucky, Louisiana, Tennessee, Mississippi, and Kansas.

Eventually, that towering structure was torn down, as the oral tradition declared "the building was haunted" because "one could still hear the cries and moans of those who were injured and had succumbed to death."

Reverend Walker left the church in 1918. Reverend Albert Garner became the second pastor, serving until 1935. The church site was rezoned for business, sold, and ultimately relocated to Fourteenth Street and Avenue G, on the city's south side. Two temporary structures, one for storage and one for worship, were constructed. The basement of the brick structure was ready for worship in 1927. God's hand was still on the church fellowship, as He marched the determined saints in and through another incredible

period of history that includes faith and fortitude, in the midst of dynamic struggles of a different type.

Years later, in 1936, Reverend Walter Wilson became the third pastor. He liquidated the church indebtedness and planned for the unfinished upper-level construction. However, the depression hit, and as was with all of America, money was extremely tight. Several factors, including but not limited to the financial woes, forced the need for the church to reorganize and become incorporated. Those reasons caused the name of the church to be changed from Shiloh to Greater Shiloh. Because of the change in name, many who have studied the history of the tragic event mentioned earlier thought the church folded or faded away in the aftermath. When God changes a church, nothing can prevent it from reaching its divine destiny.

In 1946, Reverend Allen Thomas became the fourth pastor. He was a dynamic and productive leader. The upper level of the church was completed in October of 1961. However, a new challenge rose in the face of this resilient congregation. The University of Alabama at Birmingham was sprouting its wings and its medical center was expanding. The church was forced to move again in 1969. This time, the move was from the south side of the city to the West End community, where it is currently located.

Across the years, the church has relocated four times, fluctuating from such heights as being recognized as the largest congregation in Birmingham during its years under the leadership of Reverend Walker, through periods of adversity, the Great Depression, obscurity, and low visibility within the community. However, its future looks extremely promising. Many, including me, believe that Greater Shiloh will once again become a leading presence, visible, viable, and effective in delivering witness to current and future generations.

In the 123-year storied history, there have been only five pastors. This fact alone speaks volumes concerning the stability of this church, and hints that perhaps God has maintained special plans for her. This narrative will examine the journey of this church's life from the last three years of the fourth pastor, through much of my current ministry as pastor. I will cast some visionary insights for a fifteen-year future, and chronicle what happens when God changes a church.

Inherited Circumstances

It was the second Sunday morning in December, 1985, when a thirty-one-year-old Michael Wesley first walked through the doors of Greater Shiloh, having been invited to preach at the morning worship service. Arriving at the 9:30 a.m. Sunday school study hour, I sat obscurely in the men's Bible class. Later, I introduced myself to Pastor Allen Thomas, the church's fourth pastor. He was a gracious senior gentleman, and greeted me warmly, inviting me to sit with him during the study hour and worship service.

Mrs. Lorene Pickett, a deaconess and long-time member of the church, had asked Rev. Thomas to invite me to preach at Greater Shiloh. She served as an office aide at Powderly Elementary School, where I had been appointed new principal some six months prior. She told me that her church was looking for a young minister to assist their aging pastor and explained that Rev. Allen Thomas had led them for more than thirty-five years. She quipped that now he was in his eighties and slowing down, and the church had reached an agreement with Pastor Thomas "to get him some help."

Having acknowledged God's call on my life to preach the Gospel in 1982, I was eager to preach at any opportunity that opened to me. I did not think at all about the idea of going to this church for an extended stay; only to preach and move on as I had done often during those neophyte days in the preaching ministry. However, that Sunday was special. There was an excitement in the air. The people received the Word gladly. At the conclusion of the message, "Jesus, the Reason for the Season," Pastor Thomas stood before the congregation and made a startling declaration. He relayed how the deacons had approached him, telling of the discussion and subsequent agreement they had reached regarding seeking a person to assist him. He went on to confess how at first he did not think much of the matter, and that he had reluctantly agreed. He did not think that much about the two or three ministerial candidates that had been invited to preach. However, he said, "Today, God has sent a man, brothers. There is no need to invite anyone else. God has revealed Wesley to me." The audience's response was overwhelmingly strong in agreement. I was invited back to preach on the second Sunday in February of 1986, at the Annual Men's Day observance.

After that service, a business meeting of the church was called, where the nomination to offer me the position of assistant pastor was voted on and passed unanimously. Later, the joint Boards of Deacon and Trustees formally interviewed me. An agreement was reached for me to start. The arrangements included a salary of $100.00 per Sunday. This was acceptable as I continued in my position as school principal. Duties would include assisting Rev. Thomas by assuming most of the preaching duties. Pastor Thomas would preach the first Sunday of each month, and I would preach the other three or four as the calendar dictated. Visitations to the sick were a shared responsibility. I attended board meetings, which were held at night, since Pastor Thomas did not drive after dark.

On Sunday, April 20, 1986, during an inspirational service, I was installed as assistant pastor. Nine local ministers were part of the program. My pastor, Rev. Reginald Brown, of South Elyton Baptist Church (another congregation in Birmingham), gave the installation address. He used Genesis 41:43 as the text and called the sermon "A Seat in the 2nd Chariot." The message paralleled the elevation of Joseph in Egypt as second in command to Pharaoh. More than 150 people, including many friends and well-wishers, attended and signed their names in the guest book that had been posted in the vestibule of the church.

Life at Greater Shiloh was exciting for me. It was indeed an exciting opportunity for a thirty-one-year-old young minister to listen to and learn from such a seasoned and wise pastor, and at the same time practice ministry. My wife, the former Venita Burkes of Columbus, Ohio, supported me whole-heartedly. However, it made no difference to our children Michael Jr., 4, and James Edward, 2.

My personal approach to this new opportunity was not to make any initial changes, but to try to learn about the church, the people, their relationships one to another, and the various personality types. I soon discovered that this was a family-oriented church as many churches are. I also discovered that various factions or cliques existed, and decisions were supported along those lines. Even election of church officers happened to be influenced by this same kind of mindset. Internal concerns did not leave much energy for the outreach ministry.

Greater Shiloh's presence in the community was in a period of decline, and had been for the past few years. Evidence of this truth lay in some of the following facts:

1. ***The church building was not widely used.*** It was open for the worship experience on Sunday morning, choir rehearsal on Wednesday evening, a Bible class on Saturday, and an occasional evening meeting during the week. There was no prayer service or other Bible class available.

2. As Pastor Thomas aged, ***many areas of church life faded.*** I believe this is how some of the factions began. As the pastor and his staff relinquished control over matters and management of certain areas, others gained control or stepped forward to champion different causes. For a while, it appeared that there were "little churches" within the one church. The governance of the church consisted of a pastor, who at this point was limited in decision making. The Board of Deacons and

Board of Trustees viewed themselves more as boards of control. They usually made the decisions, especially the financial ones; a biblical focus was not a part of that process. I found, to my amazement, that they held the mistaken belief that the pastor runs the spiritual side of the church and the deacons run the business side. That mentality yielded a very autocratic style of leadership within the church and produced a negative, untrusting division between the pastor and their perceived "official positions," that still exists in some form to this very day.

3. *Various auxiliaries sought to develop programs that benefitted the auxiliaries rather than the whole church.* Each group maintained its own treasury, reporting to the general treasury of the church what it willed and when. Each auxiliary unit, such as the various choirs, usher boards, and mission groups, had their own recognition day. For example, any given Sunday in the church year would be designated as #1 Choir Day, and members would be asked to support them by paying a minimal assessment of around five dollars. Also, support for these public programs depended upon whom or which group was sponsoring the activity. Consequently, there were too many annual days.

4. *Church life* was in a survival mode. Sunday worship was the primary means of visibility. Lively worship services were sporadic, usually most energetic on the second Sunday of each month when the Male Chorus sang. The Male Chorus consisted of a good group of men that were dedicated to their chorus. Joann Nabors, a gifted organist, faithfully led them, often teaching songs, encouraging men to give the music an honest try, and working miracles by getting good music out of men who didn't believe they had the talent or ability to sing. Nabors modeled a dedication that became contagious for those men. They sang a variety of the popular songs of that day, usually renditions of past and current recording artists, including Sam Cooke, The Williams Brothers, and others.

There were other choirs at the church. Each choir had an assigned Sunday to lead the worship service. The # 1 Choir, which consisted of senior adult members, sang traditional hymns and gospel tunes. They sported their own musician, Mrs. Blue, who along with her daughter, Edna, came from another church to sing and play the piano on the first Sunday of each month when the senior choir sang. This service was usually considered slow and attendance was light. The # 2 Choir, made up of young adults, was also a popular choir; they sang mostly gospel selections. The last choir, the Thomas Gospel Airs, was the youth choir named for Rev. Allen Thomas.

5. One of the most telling signs that the church was in decline was the fact *that there was no organized children's or youth ministry in those days.* Activities and ministry choices were limited. There was the youth usher board, named after one of the matriarchs of the church, Torether Mencer, who had been a no-nonsense personality, believing in strict discipline. She offered youth an opportunity to learn from her motherly wit.

The above-mentioned circumstances led me to embark on and examine my work as assistant pastor, as Rev. Thomas continued as senior pastor. Inasmuch as I attended the deacon and trustee board meetings, it was soon crystal clear to me that a biblical focus was needed to help guide the work of deacons and trustees. My approach was to address the absence of training and teaching and to foster initiatives that would generate a spirit of cooperation among the various auxiliary units. In addition, an ongoing approach to financial stewardship was essential to promote financial growth.

The financial chart on the next page depicts the financial condition of the church at this time, and shows how gradual progress began. The Sunday worship experience needed some continuity in the music department. With Rev. Thomas's sanction and approval of the deacons and trustees, I recommended ideas such as tithing and a need for a minister of music, all of which we believed would be beneficial to the congregation. It was accepted and presented to the congregation at the annual church conference meeting.

Financial Chart #1	1984	1985	1986	1987
Annual Income	$51,499.51	$53,025.56	$59,528.13	$86,496.93
Annual Expenditures	$49,481.27	$47,172.28		
Bal. On Hand	$5,649.45	$11,502.73		
Savings	$5,322.50	$6,615.00		

Some of these early recommendations would be revisited across the years of my ministry in this church. The congregation accepted a new organizational structure, and they installed a new method of reporting and recording finances for individuals and auxiliaries. Individual and general reports would be produced quarterly and annually. The new structure required all auxiliaries or groups to use the proposed new budget and requisition forms, and to report monthly on all monies from its treasure in excess of $50.00. The express purpose of this was to establish one church treasury. Now, reports were made on the fourth Sunday of each month. We reduced a large number of ineffective programs on Greater Shiloh's calendar and reduced the number of annual day celebrations to four. On these occasions, we asked members to give an offering above their regular tithes or offering.

The annual days were set:

Mission Day-4th Sunday(November)	$50.00
Men's Day-2nd Sunday (February)	$100.00
Women's Day-4th Sunday (May)	$100.00
Combined Ushers' Day–2nd Sunday (June)	$50.00
Total Each Year	$300.00

That year, I recommended some personnel and salary actions. Recommendations included creating the minister of music position, setting an annual salary for the position, and establishing a pension plan for Pastor Thomas, whose health by this time had begun to decline.

I learned quickly that quarterly church conferences were not a good thing. In October of 1986, upon my recommendation, it was approved that we would meet quarterly to monitor our progress. February of 1987 taught me better. It was to be a conference to review the first quarter's finances, and to make some additional projections. The organizational chart had been revised again. Recommendations were to be made on deacons to be ordained, men whom Rev. Thomas had decided upon some time before. In addition, I had the brilliant idea of exposing non-contributing members by having a financial statement published, which revealed the contributions of individual members.

The intent of financial transparency was not meant to embarrass. To me, it seemed like the natural thing to do. It had been done in my home church, and I did not think that anyone would find it offensive. I did not know that someone in the pre-conference deacon meeting was against such a recommendation. When the conference came, I was met with a great deal of animosity, and presented with a petition bearing the names of members who did not wish to have their names and contributions printed on a report. The meeting that I thought would be smooth turned into a rough awakening for a young assistant pastor, and I left that meeting feeling hurt and betrayed.

I started to feel the need to alter those negative feelings. Deacon meetings were more gripe sessions on minor repairs that were needed and financial reports on incidental spending. Sometimes I felt that my personal efforts were frustrated because of a lack of spiritual interest among this leadership group. Again, the church was in a maintenance mode with much energy expended within, and none on others outside the walls of the church.

Like Paul, I turned my attention from the group that would not hear me to a group that I could connect with—the youth. In June of 1987, we sponsored a three-night youth revival to try to pump some spiritual life and momentum into the congregation and community. That revival led to a youth retreat at White Sands Beach in Florida that same summer. A number of adults joined this spiritual time of renewal, which proved that more than just youth were interested.

The annual church conference in September of 1987 allowed me to reveal plans to address the spiritual needs of the membership. Those efforts with the youth drew some criticism, that perhaps too much time was being spent with one segment of the church, while other parts of the population also had needs. The objectives for the church for fiscal year 1987–88 included involving a greater number of members in church-related activities and organizations. We sought to establish mission and education ministries in the church to a place of priority. Church leadership needed to be improved throughout, from the top to the bottom. To address those needs, we developed four workshops, spread over the course of the year.

One workshop was a leadership conference for all church leaders, designed to strengthen the skills of leaders. We designed two Sunday school worker workshops to improve the teaching ability of our lay staff; a seminar for senior citizens to address practical problems of aging, and a seminar for troubled teens to address their concerns in the community. I knew we were on the right track, but it was easier to put these things on paper than it was to actually cause full buy-in. There were still pockets of resistance. This was clear, as we promoted the new financial reporting system, designed to keep members informed on how well or poorly we were moving toward meeting the approved budget. Segments of doubt troubled several people who were apprehensive that we were asking the congregation to approve more than some thought possible or practical.

Ministry was quite challenging mostly due to a lack of common focus, confusion of a biblical understanding of the church's mission, and hesitancy to embrace change. We sought multiple activities and training opportunities to inspire deacons to live closer to the biblical description of deacons. It seemed that this group of lay leaders was very autocratic and unwilling to accept the leadership of a young Joshua. Life at the church just kind of rocked on for a few years. I was not sure that I was the person for this church, so I continued to pursue advanced educational degrees, all the while making plans to fulfill what I thought was my destiny: to become a superintendent of an urban school district. However, unbeknownst to me, God had other plans. On the very day that I received a letter from Harvard University, where I had applied to pursue an educational doctoral degree in urban school superintendence, Rev. Thomas, Greater Shiloh's fourth pastor, passed away. It was then that God spoke to my heart and my mind concerning this church.

God revealed to me that He wanted me to assume leadership of this church. I was invited to accept the challenge and accepted the mantle of serving this church as senior pastor. The early years that I thought were so hard had only grown spiritual fervor within me. My passion for lost people had increased, so I continued to serve bivocational roles as senior pastor and public school educator. I served as an elementary, middle, and high school principal during these years while growing in the gifts of teaching, leadership, administration, and exhortation.

Perhaps from my work with underprivileged families, misguided youth, and many frustrated professional and semi-professional people, I realized that lost people matter to God. I had been given the privilege of serving in the three institutions that represent hope and deliverance. They are the home, the school, and the church. Truly, the trinity of hope and the foundation of society depend upon proficient performance from each of these. The success or failure of multitudes and generations lay in the hands of these institutions. Even if there is faulty parenting or no parenting in the home, God expects the lost to be found, and the school often holds the key to the avenue of escape, and a future for the underprivileged.

However, if schools fail to deliver—and they do—the church stands as the ultimate and only true beacon of hope to a hurting world. Sadly, because of the internal chaos of our local church, we were failing God and the community that surrounded us. Children and youth who were not being loved at home or supported in school needed something from us—the church—that we were not providing. Parents, some from within the community where our church is located, are often children themselves, needing guidance, direction, support, and all of the hope that the Gospel of Jesus Christ provides.

We were the "service and ministry station," but we were not functioning as we should. Armed with fresh convictions, a keen insight of the community, and the church's culture, I truly understood that a change was inevitable. I sincerely believed that as the leader of the local church, with God's help, I could take some of the mystery out of change. I was very prayerful and hopeful that we could hit a home run in making our church a winner in today's world. This would not be easy. Greater Shiloh was an old church, and I knew that the change process would be painful and slow. More importantly, if there were to be lasting change, God would have to do it.

Greater Shiloh Missionary Baptist Church
(occupied from 1969 to 2008)

PART II

God Defined the Needed Changes

Theological Underpinnings—Now, Let's Learn the Truth

When God changes a church, He does it through underscoring the critical role of the pastor and what he is to do. God wants His key person to be crystal clear about his assignment. God also wants church members to understand that assignment. In most churches, especially in the African-American tradition, members of the congregation think they know and understand the role of the pastor. There is often an adversarial implication: The pastor is to do what we say, visit our sick, bury our dead, counsel our young, and marry us when we are ready. If he is real good, we will let him preach to us once in a while.

However, God will redefine the needed understanding for both clergy and pew. He will provide clarity of the mission of His church. It does not matter whether the church is located in an urban or a rural setting. God's goal is creating understanding of the key roles and to provide a compass of the turf to be conquered. God will also expand the territory of what is possible for a church. He does this through deepening the understanding of the science of change and transition. When God changes a church, He can be trusted to educate the leader and the people.

This segment can prove invaluable to any person who desires to explore a biblical perspective on each of these matters. I am convinced that this section will help any pastor or church leader who desires clarity on God's mandate. This information will assist you in navigating the tricky waters of change.

At Greater Shiloh, we believed our church could change. We knew why we must change and sought how we were to go about that change.

First, the Bible teaches that one of the primary functions of the elder/overseer is to be a teacher for the church. The ministry of proclamation forms the foundation for the practical implementation of this ministry intervention. Second, the Scriptures indicate that a church's primary reason for existence is to be on a mission in the world. Our church had to rediscover the Great Commission, as found in Matthew 28:16-20, and its implications.

The Pastor as Teacher

When God changes a church, He uses the Scriptures to point out the role of the pastor and teacher as in the Greek construction of Ephesians 4:11-12. The phrase translated "pastor and teachers" in 4:11 uses one definite article to cover both words. This grammatical construction indicates that the terms translated as "pastors" *(poimen)* and "teacher" *(didaskalos)* are descriptive of two functions of a single congregational leader.[1] The task of the pastor and teacher, then, is "to prepare God's people for works of service, so that the body of Christ may be built up."

The pastor is to equip the whole congregation until they become mature in Christ as ministering servants. Bill Hull concisely states that the chief work of the pastor and teacher is "to bring the body of Christ to full operational efficiency through training."[2] Pastors are not to do the work of the ministry alone; they are to equip Christians to be partners with them in the great mission of the church. The pastor's gift and service to the church is to be the teacher and equipper. Pastors are to teach all things that Christ commanded (Matthew 28:20).

The ministry of proclamation should be used in significant ways. Informing the lost through preaching is a part of the equipping process. John A. Broadus defines *preaching* as the "great appointed means of spreading the good tidings of salvation through Christ."[3] Mark 1:14 informs us that proclamation is one of the principal means used to tell the Good News. The pages of the New Testament are literally filled with examples of Jesus and the apostles preaching the Good News. When pastors choose the ministry of proclamation to articulate a message for people, they are in excellent historical company.

Charles Skinner writes in the *Holman Bible Dictionary* that preaching is the "human presentation through the Holy Spirit's power of God's acts of salvation through Jesus Christ."[4] This means that the preaching event is a divine and human event. God chooses human instruments to accomplish preaching. Skinner's definition purports that God uses human beings empowered by the Holy Spirit to herald the Good News of God's mighty acts in history. J. I. Packer defines preaching as "the event of God bringing to an audience a Bible-based, Christ-related, life-impacting message of instruction and direction from Himself through the words of a spokesperson."[5]

What is the preaching mandate found in the Bible? The apostle Paul charges young Timothy in 2 Timothy 4:2 to "preach the word." The Greek word, transliterated *kerusso* and translated in the *English Bible*, means "to preach, to be a herald, proclaim." What does Paul instruct Timothy to preach? Timothy is instructed to preach the *word*, (*logos*, the Word of God). Therefore, Paul is instructing young Timothy to preach, herald, or proclaim the very Word of God.

I once heard that the task of the sermon is to describe God's unfinished agenda, in such compelling terms that the hearers will become permanently dissatisfied with the status quo. The ultimate goal of the preaching process is that Christ is formed in people. Everybody has a spirit, an inner life that is made up of emotions, the will, and the intellect. That spirit is being formed all the time. Preaching/teaching is a vital part of how Christian spiritual formation takes place in the people. We must, as one writer said, "put hay down where the goats can get it." That is the challenge. Some preachers/ teachers have hay, meaning they know theology. They know the Bible, but do not know the goats. Some know the goats but do not have any hay. The preacher/teacher must grow spiritually in order to have hay—the Word—so that people can know God.

In order for the pastor/preacher/teacher to have hay, that person must grow spiritually himself or herself. He/she must become knowledgeable of culture: people in general, their conversations, activities, and needs. The message or the talk or sermon must not be aimed to combat people in the pew; the stakes are much higher than petty, personal feuds. When God changes a church, He often causes the preacher/teacher to spend more and more time alone with Him to diminish the need of approval of the congregants he or she is trying to reach.

The Pastor as Leader

When God is actively involved in changing a church to be involved in "reaching the un-churched," not only does He prepare the pastor to understand his role as a teacher, but He also grows him or her into the leader. He molds the pastor's character. The age-old debate rages on, as to whether or not leaders are born or made. I personally believe that leaders can be made. Yes, there must be some innate or natural ability, but one can acquire the needed leadership skills and demonstrate appropriate behaviors that will elevate one as the leader. There is a difference between positional leadership and functional leadership.

In every church there are people in leadership positions who are not necessarily leaders. There are also people in every church who may not bear a title but who are leaders. Many young ministers and pastors have to learn this lesson the hard way. Many believe that because they are given the title "pastor" that everyone will automatically line up and follow them. The truth is, leading people as pastor is more about endearment than most anything else. People must learn to trust a person before they will allow that person to lead. The implied meaning is that the key to effective pastoral leadership lies in demonstrating certain consistent trustworthy behaviors.

George Barna, in his book *Leaders on Leadership*, says the central conclusion is that the "American Church is dying due to a lack of strong leadership. In this time of unprecedented opportunity and plentiful resources, the church is actually losing influence. The primary reason is the lack of leadership. Nothing is more important than leadership."[6] Barna goes on to say that the most theologically minded will immediately attack his statement and say that the most noteworthy thing is "holiness" or "righteousness" or "commitment to Christ" or "radical obedience to God." Barna says that on a theological level, he wholeheartedly agreed. However, he points out that most Americans do not live on a theological level. Since that is the case, people need to be helped. In order for anyone to become holy, righteous, committing to Christ or live radically, obediently to God, leaders are needed who will do whatever it takes to facilitate such qualities in sinful, selfish, misguided mortals.

Barna clarifies further by stating that leadership is more important on a spiritual or eternal level than our theology and spiritual commitments. He further stated that without effective, godly, Christ-honoring leadership, most people in America seem destined to a life in which Jesus Christ is little more than an expression in times of frustration or an ancient personality, irrelevant teacher of nice principles, and antiquated religious practices.

Gary Willis explains that, "Leadership is mobilizing others toward a goal shared by the leader and followers." There are five key attributes. A leader is

1. one who mobilizes.
2. one whose focus is influencing people.
3. a person who is goal-driven.

4. someone who has an orientation in common with those who rely upon him for leadership.

5. someone who has people to follow them willingly.

Writing on what makes a leader a leader, Barna highlights three distinct but related qualities: First, God calls a Christian leader, one who is called to a unique brand of servanthood. This is one who serves by leading. The vast majority of God's human creatures are followers. Those who have been anointed to lead are most valuable to the body of believers. They function by their willingness to follow their call, and to do that which followers so desperately need.

Second, a Christian leader is a person of Christlike character. The central function of a leader is to enable people to know, love, and serve God with their entire hearts, minds, souls, and strength. Therefore, the leader must possess personal attributes, characteristics of the heart, manifested through speech and behavior that reflect the nature of God.

Third, a Christian leader possesses functional competence that allows him or her to perform tasks and guide people toward accomplishing the ends intended of God's servants. These are the abilities that receive prolific attention: inspiring people, directing their energy and resources, casting vision, building teams, celebrating victories, delegating authority, making decisions, developing strategy, and accepting responsibility for outcomes.

THE CHRISTLIKE CHARACTER OF A LEADER[7]

A servant's heart	Even Tempered	Loving
Honesty	Joyful	Wise
Loyalty	Gentle	Discerning
Perseverance	Consistent	Encouraging
Trustworthiness	Spiritual depth	Passionate
Courage	Forgiving	Fair
Humility	Compassionate	Patient
Sensitivity	Energetic	Kind
Teachability	Faithful	Merciful
Values driven	Self-controlled	Reliable
	Optimistic	

THE COMPETENCIES OF A CHRISTIAN LEADER[8]

- Effective communication
- Identifying, articulating, casting vision
- Motivating people
- Coaching and developing people
- Synthesizing information
- Persuading people
- Initiating strategic action
- Engaging in strategic thinking
- Resolving conflict
- Developing resources
- Delegating authority and responsibility
- Reinforcing commitment
- Celebrating successes
- Decision making
- Team building
- Instigating evaluation
- Creating a viable corporate culture
- Maintaining focus and priorities
- Upholding accountability
- Identifying opportunities for influence
- Relating everything back to God's plans and principles
- Modeling the spiritual disciplines
- Managing other key leaders

The Church and the Mission

When God changes a church, He makes it clear what a church ought to be doing. One of the reasons for significant disparity among churches is based on what drives the church. Every church is driven by something, whether by programs (and many are), or by finances, or personalities. When God changes a church, the church is to be on a mission to this world (Matthew 28:18-20). It becomes a church that is driven by biblical purposes.

In the Bible, the Great Commission's central directive is "go and make disciples" (Matthew 28:19a). Matthew's distinctive transitive use of *matheteusate* (a Greek word translated as *make disciples*) indicates the "New Testament belief is a call for discipleship."[9] The church's mission is then to go and call out disciples from all nations by "baptizing" them and "teaching" them to observe all of Jesus' commandments. Churches do not have a choice as to what kind of church they want to be. Jesus made that decision for them. The New Testament models for today's churches are Great Commission churches. In *A History of Christian Missions*, Stephen Neill wrote, "The church of the first Christian generation was a genuinely missionary Church."[10] Today, the vital churches are those on a mission in this world. Churches exist to serve others, not just themselves. This is exactly what Greater Shiloh had to rediscover, and it is precisely what each church must learn, if it is to be all that God desires.

In today's society, many see the church as a weak, unconcerned, ineffective bunch of hypocrites. Society often views the church's function as a series of small cliques or a social club for a chosen few. Some even see the church as a miniature kingdom with selfish intentions, a place where families enjoy and select friends control. That is a far cry from the description that Bill Hybels, pastor of Willow Creek Community Church, gives to the value of a local congregation. He assesses accurately that the local church is the hope of the world. In every community from urban to rural, no matter whether village, hamlet, or metropolitan, whenever sincere Christ followers gather, they do provide the world the hope that is contained in the truth about Christ.

The English translation of the church comes from the Greek word *ekklesia* which, if taken etymologically, means *called out*.[11] When ekklesia is used in the New Testament with reference to the church, it has the connotation of the community of believers who are united by the Spirit of God. The early Christians "perceived themselves as called out by God in Jesus Christ for a special purpose."[12] When God changes a church, He is calling churches back to a historical identity of being a Great Commission church. Rick Warren states that the most important task a plateaued or declining church has is to "redefine its purpose."[13]

In *A Church for the 21st Century*, Leith Anderson puts it a little differently: "Producing disciples is what a healthy church seeks to do."[14] He further states that Matthew 28:20 defines a *disciple* as someone who obeys all that he is commanded. Perhaps Anderson's clearest statement on the church explains that "the healthy church is more concerned about glorifying God than perpetuating an organization."[15]

The Church in the Community

When God changes a church, He not only deals with the leader, the people, and their purpose, but He also then prepares that church to engage in the deeper spiritual warfare that lurks outside of its doors. Environments have long been known to wield huge influences upon individuals and entire communities of people.

A key focus in real estate sales is said to be location; it drives sales, business ventures, and investment opportunities. Zealous and/or business-savvy people look to take advantage of just the right location. That is not always the case in the life of a church. A church's location may have been predetermined by factors other than the business or growth markets that often drive many other venues. However, we must be prepared to deal with where we are. Locations can be unique, but problems, challenges, and solutions are the same no matter where we may find ourselves.

Robert Linthicum, in his book *City of God, City of Satan*, lays out the theological underpinnings of church ministry within the city. Greater Shiloh Missionary Baptist Church is located in the heart of the inner city of Birmingham, Alabama. The 35211 zip code has been cited as one of the deadliest in America. The crime rate surrounding this particular church is indeed alarming and, therefore, calls for decisive action. John Archibald is the metro columnist for *The Birmingham News*. In his February 5, 2008, column, he wrote of the intensity of crime, citing that Birmingham remained one of the deadliest cities in America during the first six months of 2007. The murder rate was five times higher than that of New York's, and the property crime rate was double that of Philadelphia's. At that time, Birmingham had the seventh-highest murder rate among U.S. cities and was ranked eighteenth in violent crime. Living within that climate, it was important for Greater Shiloh to understand the call of God for the location of our church.

Our world is becoming an urban world. This is an inevitable and irreversible trend. No previous generation has faced human problems of this magnitude, nor wielded urban power on this scale. We cannot run to relocate to rural areas or to underdeveloped areas; we must remain where God has planted us. The community needs the church's presence, vision, mission, and its ministry. We are to provide hope in the minds of citizens that need it most.

Linthicum points out from a biblical perspective that the city is the focal point of a great and continuing battle between the God of Israel, the church, and the god of the world.[16] He uses biblical passages to give us appropriate insight.

In the Old Testament, the God of Israel may be called Yahweh. In the New Testament, He is the *God of our Lord and Savior, Jesus Christ.* In the Old Testament, the god of the world may be named *Baal.* In the New Testament, he is called Satan. It does not matter whether God is called Yahweh or the Father of Jesus Christ, whether the Evil One is called Baal or Satan, the overarching message is the same. This world is a battlefield. The greatest battle goes on in our cities: the battle between God and Satan.

It is a fight for both the people and systems of human society. Behind the seduction of a city's systems and structures, behind the principalities and powers that form the spiritual essence of those systems, is often a dark and destructive angel who broods over the city seeking to possess it. Behind these stands the shadowy figure known as Satan. It is the "father of lies" who is at both the heart and the head of a city's seduction.

Linthicum probes the question of "what are the marks of truly effective urban ministry?" He poses four more questions that reveal transformative answers:

- Are the systems of a city being confronted and offered real potential for change?

- Are the poor and exploited of the city provided the vehicles by which they can bring about change in their situation?

- Are the middle class and the powerful given the opportunity to join in common cause with the poor to confront the systems of the city and seek their transformation?

- Is there a spiritual transformation that is going on in that city, or is the change only social? Are the lives both of that city's poor and of the powerful being changed?

Linthicum then raises another question: "Is there in Scripture an example of an urban ministry which exhibits these four marks of truly effective ministry?" The answer is yes. Nehemiah's ministry confronted the city's systems and saw significant transformation occur. This ministry organized the people of that city—both its poor and its powerful—to reverse the destructive directions of that city. A result of this ministry was a profound spiritual transformation, not only of the city itself, but also of an overwhelming majority of its people. This ministry of presence, prayer, practice, and proclamation exposed the lies of the powers that would have exploited that city, and it engaged the people in creating for themselves a new vision of what it meant for them to be "the city of God." This vision was so profound that it altered for a time the self-understanding and mission directions of the Jewish people.

The whole world belongs to God—including the city. It was made by God's hand, for God placed in humanity the capacity to create the city. The thing God wants most for the city is that God's people, the church, will be humble of heart, contrite, and cognizant of their own sins. We should not, therefore, condemn those in the cities who are marginalized, who are poor, or powerless, or without hope. God wants a people who can tremble in awe, both at the work God would do in that city, and at the recognition that they are called to be a part of that great work. It is incumbent upon Christians today to recognize and enthusiastically enter into the challenge of the new, emerging world. God is calling the church into the city. This means that the church has unprecedented potential for ministry and world evangelization. The world is coming to the city. We can be there to greet them in Christ's name.

God planted the church in the community on the Day of Pentecost approximately AD 33. It is a living organism designed to make "Christ" known to the world. The church has marched from the day of her beginning throughout the centuries to the present time, waving the banner of salvation through Christ in the faces of each generation.

The church, the body of baptized believers, is said to be "the salt of the earth," and as such, is a preserver of society. Its presence, through its messages and ministry, affects the lives of the citizens of its day. The message influences the philosophy or belief system of people in such a profound way. Human conduct in daily living is altered. The result is changed lives. The church's presence retards the decay of the world and delays final judgment until God's appointed time. The church is to trumpet divine truth to the world through its community presence and ministry. The church will continue its presence in the world until Jesus returns to rapture the saints. At that time her warfare would be over and in the language of the old Negro Baptist Church, "the old ship of Zion would have landed many a thousand" safely on the harbors of eternity.

In neighborhoods, communities throughout the world, from jungle villages to principal metropolitan cities, churches stand as warriors of faith. Our vocation or profession is to be God's transformed people. The church is to be the sign, example, and dealings (in word and deed) of God's reclamation work. We are to show Christ among people, cities, nations, systems, structures, principalities, and powers. We are to be, in our actions, our words, and our lives together, models of the people we claim to be.

In Ephesians 4, Paul introduces three threats to being the church. He does not suggest that we avoid these threats, because we cannot. They are inevitable manifestations of the enemy in any church seeking seriously to live in harmony. Rather than asking how we may avoid these threats, we need to ask how we may deal with them when they raise their ugly heads.

The three threats to the church's life in the community noted in Ephesians 4 are (1) conflict between Christians (verses 1-6), (2) diversity of gifts and services (verses 7-13), and (3) heresy and unorthodox teaching (verses 14-16). To these three threats the church should apply the principles of unity (verses 1-6), peace (verses 7-13), and purity (verses 14-16).[17] First, conflict between Christians threatens the church's life in the community. Divisive conflict undermines the church as it tries to live in the community and exposes the talk of the community as a lie. The answer to such divisiveness and conflict is unity based on the Spirit.

It is a unity that must be conscientiously practiced. Paul writes, "Be completely humble and gentle; be patient, bearing with one another in love" (verse 2). Being the church requires us to be tolerant of one another, to be selfless, gentle, patient—not to take umbrage, but put up with what is irritating in each other.

It is a unity that must be accentuated. Paul writes, "Make every effort to keep the unity of the Spirit through the bond of peace" (verse 3). Tolerating each other and overlooking the annoying are not enough. We must seek to preserve our unity; we must work for our peace. It requires intentional effort.

It is a unity that must be based on affirmation of our common faith. The apostle states, "There is one body and one Spirit—just as you were called to one hope when you were called—one Lord, one faith, one baptism; one God and Father of all, who is over all and through all and in all" (Ephesians 4:4-6).

Second, a diversity of gifts and service (Ephesians 4:7-13) can threaten the church's life in living in unity. Paul writes, "But to each one of us grace has been given as Christ apportioned it. It was He who gave some to be apostles, some to be prophets, some to be evangelists, and some to be pastors and teachers, to prepare God's people for works of service, so that the body of Christ may be built up until we all reach unity in the faith and in the knowledge of the Son of God and become mature, attaining to the whole measure of the fullness of Christ" (verses 7, 11-13).

Diversity does not mean division. In order for the church to function effectively both as a community and institutionally, Paul tells us, "God has given a diversity of gifts to it." Some of these gifts are gifted people in the form of pastors and teachers. Their functions make up the diversity of gifts, and behind such gifts is an even broader diversity of service.

The danger in this biblical principle for organizing the life of the church is human pride. Behaviors such as jealousy, hunger for prestige, mistrust, resentment, and envy can come creeping in without warning. Rather than celebrating, fully living into the ministry and gifts that God has given us individually, it is easy to begin envying the gifts of others and their positions of respect and prestige in the church. When that disease infects the entire life of a congregation, it can destroy that body through suspicion, resentment, and greed.

The purpose for the diversity of gifts must be stressed. All the gifts given to the body exist for only one purpose: to enable the entire community of faith to undertake effectively its "work of service." Only in this way does the "body of Christ get built up," "the unity of the faith" gets practiced, the knowledge of Christ becomes deepened, and the entire community becomes a mature community that is the actualized body of Christ.

Recognition for the "lesser" works of service must be stressed so that some people do not feel inferior. Paul recognized the inherent danger in his principle of the diversity of gifts. So he asserts in a comparable passage that the eye cannot say to the hand, "I don't need you!" The head cannot say to the feet, "I don't need you!" On the contrary, those parts of the body that seem to be weaker are indispensable, and the parts we think are less honorable should be treated with distinct honor. God has combined the members of the body and has given greater honor to the parts that lacked it, so that there should be no division in the body, but that its parts should have equal concern for each other. "If one part suffers, every part suffers with it; if one part is honored, every part rejoices with it" (1 Corinthians 12:21-26).

Unity is critical; Paul teaches in 1 Corinthians that if you do not want to have dissent, jealousy, and bitterness in your church, you had better find some effective way to bring recognition of those people who are called to the church's less prestigious tasks. People in such positions have every bit as much need to be honored and recognized as do people in pivotal positions—perhaps even more.

Third, heresy and unorthodox teaching (Ephesians 4:14-16) threaten the church's life in the community. Paul writes, "Then we will no longer be infants, tossed back and forth by the waves, and blown here and there by every wind of teaching and by the cunning and craftiness of men in their deceitful scheming" (verse 14).[18]

Paul uses several metaphors here. A church which does not practice purity of doctrine, and is deficient in its teaching agency, can be likened to children led astray easily. Children do not use discernment. In the same way, a church can be likened to a boat out of control, on a wild and storm-tossed sea; both lack control. Also, both need a reliable, steady hand at the tiller. A church can be likened to a magician who has an audience; through his or her craft, the magician is able to persuade people to believe what is not so. That is the responsibility of the magician—to make the difficult to believe believable.

A church must be surefooted in theory and clear about the substance of one's faith. This is as effective as the peaceful use of the diversity of a church's gifts and the implementation of its unity.

Greater Shiloh was experiencing some of these real issues prior to our mission to submit to God's complete control. To be honest, occasional hints of old behaviors surface even now. New members are constantly joining and new offenses continue to be committed. Human nature has remained unchanged. I'm sure that many churches face these issues and do not have a way to address them. I may also indicate that it is not easy to correct errors in judgment, as it often remains anonymous. Error will not be removed overnight. In our church, there were elements of conflict, a lack of knowledge concerning the variety of and proper use of spiritual gifts coupled with dangerous levels of pride in individuals, jealousy, and a lack of awareness of the valuable contributions of persons not viewed as significant as others. There was a lack of conviction and a lack of commitment to some of the commonly perceived perspectives about the faith. A change had to be made. A change did occur. God changed His Church. He changed His sons and daughters, His family, and He continues to work on us.

Transition Issues—Here Comes Change

"To improve is to change; to be perfect is to change often."

~Winston Churchill

When God changes a church to be a church reaching the un-reached it involves both scientific and theological processes. Some changes are natural, and some are supernatural. The person or persons responsible for guiding a church during such periods would be wise to be informed by those who specialize in this area of thought. As God has changed Greater Shiloh, we have found ourselves right in the middle of trying to manage our transitions. This segment provides a backdrop of understanding what was going on in our local congregation not so much from me providing here a blow-by-blow account of what was taking place, but from the insights provided by some of America's noted change management experts such as William Bridges, Craig Satterlee, William Easum, and many others. My hope is that not only our church family but also anyone interested in the science of leadership and change can glean insight from this section.

Most pastors and church leaders have surface knowledge concerning transformation. Most are spoiled; we want our way and when things do not go our way we are often hurt, frustrated, or frightened. Some of those negative feelings could be brought under control if there was a better understanding of the territory. These include awareness of the difference between the following:

- change and transition;
- managing transitions;
- resistance to transitions; and
- the processes involved in transitions.

As these matters are clarified for you in this section of research, allow yourself to be stretched by concepts that will lead to a more balanced approach to change in your world, and perhaps less frustration as you work through them.

William Bridges in his national best seller, *Managing Transitions: Making the Most of Change*, says that it is essential to distinguish between change and transition.[19] Craig Satterlee in his book, *When God Speaks Through Change*, further quotes Bridges explaining that, "change is situational." Situations arise that change the congregation. Some examples are these: the largest employer in town announces layoffs; or the congregation no longer reflects the neighborhood surrounding the church building; or the congregation unexpectedly receives a $2 million contribution.

A congregation's success at responding to any change ultimately depends upon the congregation's willingness to claim a new identity and adopt new ways of responding to the new situation. When congregations fail to claim new identities and adopt new ways of responding to change, ministries stall and become less relevant; congregational life deteriorates.[20]

Congregational transition is the process of reshaping a group's trust foundation, their new identity, and new ways of being that result from a new situation. Whereas change is situational or physical, transition is a psychological or mental journey from the congregation's traditional role to an identity fitting the truth brought on by a physical change. Transition is the process by which a congregation comes to terms with layoffs in its community. A congregation can adapt or fail to adapt to its changing neighborhood. Also, a congregation must determine how it will minister as a faith people if suddenly there were substantial changes in financial resources. All congregations experience changes that alter their faith principles, identity, and ways of being. How congregations manage the transitions determines the nature of their life and ministry in the new reality.[21]

When congregations are not clear on these matters and confuse the difference between change and transition, the outcomes and the roles of resolving the issue are also cloudy. For example, a congregation that cannot meet its budget may assess all of its ministries in terms of its financial "bottom line" to solve the problem. Unfortunately, when a congregation approaches change in this manner, the situation becomes more complicated as the group's enthusiasm, energy, and ability to perform diminish.

On the other hand, when a congregation approaches a change as initiating a transition, the congregation itself becomes the focus. The starting point in a change is not finding the answer to the problem. The starting point is identifying what the congregation needs to let go of and the ending that the congregation needs to make. The budget deficit serves as an indication that the congregation needs to let go of things as they increase their mission and relationship to the community they serve. It is only by making this ending that the congregation can move into the new reality brought on by the change. Adapting to this new reality is a process in which the congregation embraces the change in such a way that it can become something different.

The implementations of these truths were germane to our local congregation. One will need only to look at what began to take place inside of the ministry since the year 2000. We began to implement a different mindset about how we were going to go about doing church ministry. Those mental transitions have been extremely slow, and in some cases painful. We had to alter some long-standing practices and define leadership roles differently.

Look at how change impacted the church after November 30, 2008, the date the church relocated to a new facility. We moved from a building of 9,000 square feet to one of 37,000 square feet. We moved from an obscure location within the community to an area of high visibility, onto a main artery that runs through the district from east to west. Our congregation went through both a change and a transition. The contributing factors included an increase in financial responsibility, large numeric growth, and dear old-fashioned human resistance to change. The larger the congregation becomes the more excellent everything must be.

The changes encapsulated by the terms, post-modernity, post-Christendom, and post-denominationalism compel Christian leaders increasingly to conclude that congregational life, like life itself, is not fixed. Pastors today need to understand that all of ministry is temporary. The truth is that congregational life is an ongoing process composed of overlapping transitions.

Instead of initiating transitions, changes, or crises into the life of a congregation, pastors must learn to adjust the pace and intensity transitions that are already and always ongoing. From this perspective, the first task in leading congregations in development is not anticipating the next version, but sorting through and identifying the present changes that are continually occurring in the congregation's life.

Joseph Jeter, professor of homiletics at Brite Divinity School at Texas Christian University, asserts that three types of crises tend to interrupt an orderly homiletic agenda: public, congregational, and personal.[22] Public crises include political crises and natural and other kinds of disasters. Congregational crises affect a particular local church. Personal crises go directly at members of the congregation, people in the community, and even the preacher. All three types of change have the potential to launch a congregational transition.[23]

Craig Satterlee also says that we might also describe changes that cause congregational transitions by whether they originate outside or within the congregation. For example, the process of creating and embracing a new vision for mission is itself a change initiated by the congregation itself. We might also consider the nature of the change. Some changes are unexpected and unwanted; others anticipated and welcomed. While change can be traumatic with obvious long-term consequences, it can also be slow and delicate with unclear implications. Finally, the changes that bring on congregational transition are both unpredictable and part of a group's normal development. These changes may be temporary or permanent.

In and of itself, change is neutral. Any change can be approached as either a threat or an opportunity, either a cause for celebration or a reason to despair. The issue confronting congregations and their leaders are not the changes themselves. The issue is the congregation's response to both the change and the transition it initiates. People instinctively resist transitions for two reasons. First, people naturally fight to keep their domain and the meaning and recognition they get through it. Even a positive change threatens the world of meaning and identity. In many congregations, denial is a favorite resistance. Leaders need to address the threat to the people's world of meaning posed by the change. People reduce resistance to change when leaders address perceived threats.

The second reason congregations resist change is that, ideally, they do not want to enter into a new world of meaning and identity until everyone is comfortable with it. Keeping the community, and avoiding further disagreement among members of the congregation, is the root of a congregation's desire to resist until everyone is on board.

Resistance is a way of giving people time to feel at ease with the new reality. Unfortunately, change comes so fast today in every area of life, that people have less and less time to get comfortable. In fact, in many areas of congregational life, transition and the new world of meaning and identity that it brings, cannot be delayed until everyone is of one accord. This pressure to move quickly is extremely difficult because many people rely on their congregation to be a place of permanence and stability in an ever-changing world. Many communities of faith also go to extraordinary lengths both to honor every opinion and avoid conflict that may result from moving in any way with less than full consensus.

Leaders must make it their priority to help people understand and "own" problems brought on by the change as necessary, urgent, and solvable, before attempting to introduce and implement solutions. The journey from understanding and owning the problem to initiating and implementing a solution is one way of envisioning a congregational transition; the dynamics of transition make for a long and difficult journey. Bringing the congregation through the transition that results from change is essential to its faith, community, mission, and life as the members find themselves in a new reality.

All across this nation, within the congregational life of churches, the changes brought on by a postmodern world, a post-Christian culture, and a post-denominational church have caused severe transitions in theological understanding, doctrine, Christian practice, and the church's position in society—so profound that many pastors regard change as a normal and an expected part of parish ministry. Despite the assumptions held by many congregations, the diverse forms of religion, competing value systems, and privatized Christianity that characterize modern society reveal that if American culture was ever truly "Christian," that time has passed. Finally, although denominational labels once defined congregational life, today, people make decisions to join faith communities based on how well their spiritual needs are met.[24]

William Bridges defines *transition* as a three-phase process that people go through as they internalize and come to terms with the new situation that a change brings about.[25] Bridges labels these three phases "Ending," "Neutral Zone," and "New Beginning." He uses the term *phases* to describe these three elements, possibly giving the impression that they are stages, periods of time, or like chapters in a book. Leaders of congregational transition make clear that Bridges's model is useful for understanding congregational transitions when the three parts—Ending, Neutral Zone, and New Beginning—are understood not as phases, but as threads or strands woven into the tapestry of the congregation's life.

In every transition things end. Congregations must let go of at least part of their old identity and ways of doing things—even when changes are welcomed. For example, when a congregation moves into its own church building, it must give up both its nomadic identity and its tradition of unpacking before worship and packing up afterward. Letting go is more difficult. The things the congregation must relinquish are often the exact things that got the congregation where it is. When it reaches a certain size, a congregation that understands itself as a "close-knit family" must let go of and change its identity, if it is to continue to grow.

The problem, of course, is that people do not like endings and the losses that they bring. Therefore, the primary responsibility in dealing with this strand of transition is to help people deal with their losses and to challenge their denial. People who drag their feet, resist, and sabotage have clear and valid reasons for doing so, at least from their perspective. An ending requires that leaders discover what those reasons are and address them.

While Bridges labels the second phase of transition the Neutral Zone, Craig Satterlee prefers to call it the liminal strand.[26] From the Latin *limen*, or threshold, this liminal strand is an in-between time when the past is gone, but the new has not fully arrived. The liminal phase takes place in time, space, or both time and space, and can take months or even years. During this time, people experience limited separation from established roles, status, and behavior. Since old structures are passing away and new structures are not yet established, people start structures specific to the liminal phrase and use them to deconstruct and restore identity and ways of being and doing, so that the fundamental psychological realignments and reshaping take place in both individuals and the corporate culture. The provisional and temporary nature of liminality leads many researchers to compare it to death, to being in the womb to invisibility, darkness, the wilderness, and an eclipse of the moon or sun.

Yet liminality is not the wasted and useless time that it often seems to be. The liminal strand of development is a time of reorientation and redirection. The deconstruction and reconstruction of traditional ways of doing and being can restore enthusiasm. It can also provide people room to support new initiatives that result in inspired words and actions. Questions can lead to breakthrough answers. Chaos is more amenable to new ideas than methods and routines.[27]

The problem inherent in this strand of transition is that separation from established roles, status, and behavior causes people's anxiety to increase, and their determination to fall. They tend to withdraw, becoming less frequent in worship and less involved in congregational life. Old wounds in the company's history reopen, and old weaknesses reemerge. People are overloaded. They may become polarized. The congregation becomes more vulnerable to attack from outside when neighboring congregations begin to look healthier and more attractive. Members often feel the danger inherent in this strand of transition. Many attempts to rush through or to move out of fear fail. However, when members view change as an opportune time, they develop the proper understanding. The liminal strand has the potential to be the most creative period in the transition.

Congregational leaders undertake three tasks to make the liminal feature a creative opportunity rather than a frightening wasteland:

1. Provide enough discipline to get people through in one piece.

2. Capitalize simultaneously on the confusion of the liminal strand by encouraging innovation, promoting experimentation, seeking new solutions to old problems, and embracing failures as valuable.

3. Resist the desire for certainty and closure. Congregations often try too fast to "get back to normal" when there is no "normal" place to return to. Resisting people's desire for certainty and closure is continuous.

The third strand in the transitional process is a new beginning. This is the time when the congregation develops its new identity, experiences new life, and discovers the new direction and sense of purpose, which allows it to pass into its new reality. New beginnings characterize new understandings, new attitudes, new values, new identities, or a combination of any of these. The challenge inherent in this strand of transition is that people want new beginnings to happen, but at the same time fear them. New beginnings trigger old anxieties and involve risk. They force people to come to terms with both the possibility of failure and the impossibility of returning to the way things were; this recognition may conjure up a sense of nostalgia that has the potential to delay or derail the new beginning. Finally, new beginnings are frightening because they stop what was for some a pleasant experience—the spontaneity and chaos of the liminal strand.[28]

Congregations cannot assume that new beginnings will happen automatically. In fact, congregational transitions often lack commitment, both in the congregation and the heart and spirit of the preacher, even years later. For example, the circumstances surrounding a pastor's decision to leave a congregation may cause both the pastor and the congregation to second guess long after the decision is made. Similarly, congregations that do not arrive at the new beginnings they hoped and planned for may never understand why. Since new beginnings are not automatic, a step-by-step plan requires phasing in the new reality. This plan needs to be carefully designed and implemented; it must be carefully nurtured as it unfolds. Successful plans for implementing new beginnings include at least three components.

First, it is necessary to explain the basic purpose for the new beginning that the congregation seeks. The purpose must be right, not obscure or make-believe. Initiating a new beginning to be a "faithful," "missional," "vital," or "growing" congregation is too vague. Increasing membership by 200 people in the next two months is probably unrealistic. The purpose for a new beginning must arise out of the congregation's will, abilities, and resources, and from the way these characteristics interact with the congregation's current status. The congregation will recognize that the new beginning is both possible and definite.

The second component of a successful strategy for phasing in a new beginning is the creation of a picture, or image, of how the congregation will look and feel in the new reality. The impression in people's heads is the reality in which they live. Images, therefore, have the ability to create real change in people, lift them into truth, and move them beyond themselves.[29]

Fred Craddock argues that before the creation of a new identity and new behavior, images must be replaced, and this can be done only gradually, by other images.[30] Even before new images form in people's minds, they change identity and behavior by challenging traditional images that are inadequate, inaccurate, or incomplete. In addition to addressing people individually, common vision forms in a group through viewing pictures of a new beginning. Walter Brueggemann, professor emeritus of Old Testament at Columbia Theological Seminary, Decatur, Georgia, reminds us of the power of images to move us outward (beyond the world that we know) by embodying an alternative vision of reality and giving us another world to enter.[31] In determining the picture of the new beginning, we must take care not to overwhelm people with an image that is intimidating rather than stimulating.

The third component in a successful strategy for making a new beginning is inviting participation. Allow many members roles in the plan and the new reality. Giving people something to do reassures them that they continue to be important, that they have a role in the new beginning, and that they will not be forgotten, left behind, or excluded. Leaders must be intentional to invite people who lost something significant in the transition to be a part of the emerging reality.

Leaders must do more than tell the congregation why the change is needed. Leaders need to involve as many people as possible in the transition. Widespread participation gives more members convincing, firsthand experience of the problems that make letting go and beginning anew necessary. For example, the move toward building expansion, necessitated by a crowded Sunday school, is much more palatable to those who have spent time teaching. Involving as many people as possible in the new beginning also makes the congregation and its leader allies rather than adversaries, and helps everyone to become invested in the success of the new beginning.

While Bridges's model is helpful for understanding congregational transitions, it is, like all models, limited in some significant ways. First, rather than simply following a three-step process, one must assume that congregational transitions are complex and demand multilayered events. Analyzing congregational transitions is more like looking through a kaleidoscope than at a series of slides. However desperately congregations may need a plan to guide them, rarely do they get landmarks on the journey of transformation that signals the end of one phase and the beginning of another. Sometimes a congregation's choices and decisions make it difficult to find the ending or new beginning. Rather than a clearly defined procedure, transition is an ongoing journey in which endings, liminal phases, and beginnings all blend into one another and occur simultaneously in different areas of the congregation's life. The consultants and Satterlee speak of the parts of transition as strands rather than steps for this reason.

Second, a congregational transition is rarely an isolated occurrence. One congregational transition brings on more transitions. When a pastor leaves, a congregation often reconsiders its mission, finances, and organizational plan. Congregational transitions can also initiate personal transitions in the pastor and other leaders, congregational groups, and individuals in the congregation. Completing one transition may initiate another.

When congregations experience multiple transitions whether simultaneously or over time, "transition fatigue" is an essential but often overlooked factor that needs to be addressed by leaders. Transition fatigue describes the weariness and resistance that often results from the piling up of many transitions. Leaders, therefore, must be careful to allow proper spacing to occur between transitions by causing delays, duel tracking, or other methods to keep fatigue from occurring. One example of causing a delay would be a church losing a pastor, and all the processes that would follow that experience. The church would, for example, set up a search committee to find a new leader. Delays for a year or more could be created in such situations, allowing for proper adjustments to take place before bringing in someone new.

Third, congregational transitions are unpredictable. A transition may turn out to have an impact far beyond what we expect. Sometimes what a congregation thinks of as the transition turns out not to be the actual transition. The course and direction of a transition can change quickly. People's perceptions and reactions rarely remain stable over time. Attentive listening to the congregation, flexibility, and a willingness to amend the transitional plan are, therefore, essential ingredients for successfully leading a congregation through transition.

Fourth, congregational transition involves more than abstract cognition and emotions. Congregational transitions have concrete dimensions that can be measured in time and space. Leading congregations in transition requires paying attention to such physical concerns as geography, congregational space, and the physical health and well-being of those making the transition.

Finally, congregational transitions always affect people's relationship with God. In every transition, congregations consider God's nature, purpose, and participation in light of the prevailing situation. Is God an anchor or a breeze? Is God comforting, challenging, punishing, or abandoning the congregation? What is God calling the congregation to do? What is this situation and this transition? Why are they happening? What is God's purpose, or is there a reason at all? To help congregations come to terms with these questions, preachers need to consider how they and their congregations might reflect theologically on the journey of transition.[32]

Theological Reflection on Transition
Scholars Weigh In on Change

In times of transition, our notions of God's nature, God's future, and our place in that future are often threatened. Those who dare to preach and to lead in times of congregational change must themselves come to terms with God's position and role in change. Reflecting theologically on change leads us to ask such questions as

- Who does God show Himself to be in the midst of transition?

- Does God create change, protect us from change, or empower us to respond to change?

- How do we, amid change, let God be God for the congregation and the pastor?

- How do we know if a given change and transition are of God?

- How can we be certain of God's will and direction for us?

Ronald J. Allen, professor of Preaching and New Testament at Christian Theological Seminary in Indianapolis, suggests that from a theological perspective, change and transition will cause people of faith to experience two types of crises: crises of understanding and crises of decision.[33] Crises of understanding occurs when people question the existence, identity, and nature of God. Confronted by a crisis of understanding, people often find themselves lost in a spiraling stream of consciousness in which one unanswered question leads to another. For example, people may ask

- Is God all-knowing, all-powerful, and all-loving? If so, how could this crisis have happened? Since this did happen, what does that say about God's nature?

- Could God have intervened to minimize or even prevent this?

- Could we have done something to persuade God to intervene?

- Do we know what that is?

- Why would God need to be persuaded?

- If God could intervene, why did not God intervene?

- If we could do something to convince God to intervene, why didn't we?

People question God's will in the crisis. They also question God's existence. When God does not seem to operate in the way people think, they often question the truth of God's mere existence.

A decision crisis develops when people do not know how to respond when they are unavoidably confronted with the unknown. These situations and issues escalate into a crisis of decision when people do not have time to consider their response to the following circumstances: When the way they want to respond differs from the way they know they should respond; when they confront circumstances different from anything they have previously encountered and have no precedent to guide them.

Although we have discussed crises of understanding and crises of decision separately, Allen reminds us that they are inseparably linked. Our understanding of God influences and may even determine how we respond to crisis, change, and transition. We respond one way if we trust a God who is with us in suffering, bringing life out of death and light out of darkness. We respond another way if convinced that God is distant, indifferent, or even dead. We respond a third way if we conclude that the crisis, change, or transition is the result of divine activity and judgment.

From a theological perspective, our understanding of God shapes how we decide to respond to change, crisis, and transitions. On some level, a crisis of decision results from a crisis of understanding. If our basic understanding of God as faithful, loving, and present remains unshaken by change and transition, we will be able to discern and decide how to respond. At the same time, we recognize that change and transition will nuance, refine, challenge, and enrich this foundational understanding of God.

Transitions Biblically
The Bible Has Its Say

As we strive to respond to crises of understanding and decision, telling the story of the congregation's progress by means of biblical images and narratives helps to connect the issue to God's ongoing work of salvation. The stories of the Bible affirm that God's work of salvation is changing, involving an end, an in-between time, and a new beginning. One biblical example includes God's leading Israel out of slavery in Egypt, through the wilderness into the Land of Promise. Paul's journey from Jerusalem to Damascus is another. Jonah's time in the belly of the fish is an in-between incident that marked an end and a new beginning in Jonah's ministry, as is Jesus' encounter with a Canaanite woman from the region of Tyre and Sidon (Matthew 15:21-28).

The range of biblical stories and images that connect with a change are vast and suggests various ways of approaching both Scripture and the congregational transition. Leaders and congregations in progress who read the Bible through the lens of transition, and reach the transition trusting the God revealed in Scripture, automatically find new insights, perspectives, and possibilities for moving forward. Preachers and congregations might begin by turning to the lectionary and their favorite Bible stories. Then, recognizing that both congregations and faith traditions have cherished Bible stories and images, we all need to expand our use of the biblical story and metaphor to achieve even greater appreciation. For when we read the Bible through the lens of transition, allowing Scripture to form our judgment as well as our response, both our favorite stories and many others reveal a God who continually transforms the world. It reveals a God who will not quit on us until the whole world conforms to the life He intends.

Using the language of the Bible to speak of and reflect on the congregation's action also helps the preacher and followers to understand that as the people of God, they are by faith and calling an unsettled people. Experiencing change, receiving new insight and understanding, and embracing a new call and direction are all normal and expected parts of the life of faith. Congregations must understand themselves as changing people. However, transitions can make congregations and their leaders suspicious of God. God prepares congregations with each step as preparation for another. In such situations, it is useful for congregations and their leaders to communicate to rediscover that God has always provided for the congregation.

Faith communities have hope because they have seen how God provides. They are also reminded that, as God's people, we do not need to find God in transition; God always finds us. Even the prophet Elijah went looking for God in a time of personal crisis. He did not find God in the earthquake, wind, and fire. Instead, God found Elijah in a still small voice (1 Kings 19:1-18).

As a congregation seeks to discern God's will, His approach is normally the difficult choice. Congregations may find that the most reliable way to connect the move is also the more complex one. A declining assembly may decide to forgo the struggle to regain viability. Instead, they may choose the difficult path of completing its ministry as a tangible witness to the new life that God will bring out of the congregation's death. Today, the church increasingly hears the need to respond to betrayals of trust by church leaders by choosing the difficult path of openness and candor.

Finally, Charles Campbell's book, *The Word Before the Powers*, provides theological insight into opposition in transition. Bridges's statement of transition suggests that people's struggle in a transition can be traced to fear, the sense of loss, a lack of understanding, or a lack of ownership. Bridges makes the case that leaders overcome resistance by discovering the reasons people resist and address them. However, Campbell's work suggests that resistance to change is more than the consequence of the psychological state of the congregation or the incompetence or mismanagement of its leaders. He says competition in transitions (and preaching) may be due in part to the participation of the powers and principalities—that is, the powers of death at work in the world. Campbell argues that the world's powers and principalities act aggressively in subtle but deadly ways. They influence human life today and provide the context for Christian preaching.[34]

William M. Easum, noted author and president of 21st Century Strategies, Inc., in an article entitled, "Turning a Church Around Is a Dangerous Calling," said church transformation takes a minimum of five years.[35]

At the dawn of the new millennium, Greater Shiloh was facing a lot of uncertainty. The world approached the year 2000 with many uncertain possibilities. The nations of the world feared that key computers would crash, and other catastrophic events of destruction would take place. We were facing a world where no one knew what anything would look like. We were entering a world in which more and more adults had never been inside the door of an institutional church. Change was in the air. In spite of all of the uncertainty that was in the world, our congregation was entering into transitioning from the old to the new. The transformation of our church is still under way. However, from the start, I knew we were going to face quite a storm of protest. We are an old, historic church. Change is always slow; the older a church is, the slower the changes will be in manifesting themselves.

Strong biblical preaching and teaching has always been my forte. One way to approach this wave of change was to prove 1 Corinthians 9:22 to our people: "I will become all things to all people in order to win some." For a while, that passage of Scripture was our theme. I found enough inspiration in 1 Chronicles 12:32, which highlights the fact that the men of Issachar, whom God gifted, offered their expertise to the new King David, to understand the times and know what Israel should do. I did not know all of what to do, but I knew that we had to do something different, so I became passionate in my praying and a diligent student of change.

I became a project manager and guided a Bible study that blossomed into comprehensive, strategic planning. That strategic planning process became the eye-opening experience and springboard to introduce us to analytical methods. The result led to consistent biblical purpose going on in our church.

Business expert Joel Barker says a principled leader often develops instincts and intuition of what works and what does not work. The same holds true in ministry. Dale Galloway, former dean of Asbury Theological Seminary's Beeson International Center for Biblical Preaching and Church Leadership, has provided some valuable insights on church transitions. In his article, "Taking the Mystery Out of the Change Process," he lists "ten change realities" that he believes helps in our understanding of the change process[36]:

1. There is no such thing as an unchanging church. He explains that all living organisms, whether plants, animals, or people, are subject to the phenomenon of life cycles. Living things are born, grow, age, and die. The same is true for the church. It is always changing either for better or worse.

2. Without change there is no change. Common sense says that it is folly to do the same thing over and over while expecting different results. Dale Galloway quotes Sam Shoemaker, the Episcopal priest involved in the founding of Alcoholics Anonymous, when he asked, "Can your kind of church change your kind of world?" If it cannot, it must change in order to become effective in today's world.

3. There is no change without some discomfort and pain. Human nature avoids most kinds of misery, but wise leaders know how to manage their followers as they lead them into the unknown.

4. Perception becomes reality. It may not be fair or just, but if something becomes a church's belief, it is as strong as truth.

5. What people do not understand, they will be against. Often, opposition simply means that people have not identified the concept behind or benefits of a proposed change.

6. The reason the change is uncomfortable is it usually means giving up something of the past. In the eyes of many people, change is equal to a loss.

7. Change is a process. Improving quality requires a comprehensive culture change. Dale Galloway on John Maxwell said that people change in three environments: "when they hurt enough that they have to change," "when they learn enough that they want to change," or "when they receive enough that they are able to change."

8. It is not change that will do you in, it is the transition. Galloway refers to William Bridges's work, *Managing Transition*, where he notes that it is the transition period, not the change itself, that is the

problem. Change is external, transition internal. Change does not equal transition. Again, change is situational: the new boss, new team role, and new policy. Transition is the psychological process people go through to come to terms with new situations.

9. Not everyone will adapt to change at the same rate. Everett Rodgers's book, *Diffusion of Innovations*, contains a widely reprinted chart that shows how people respond to a new idea. A few jump on early, but many wait until after the majority has adopted it. Each personality needs a different level of knowledge and support. People may resist change initially, but eventually most can adapt to it.

10. A method of ministry that works successfully in one church or region may not work in another. It is essential for the pastor to know the region's culture as well as the church's culture. Often they are distinctly different. The implication is that even if some ministry activity worked well in one's town, there is no guarantee that the same action will work well in one's church.[37]

A church congregation needs to be constantly reminded and sold on the ways in which change needs to happen to get to where God is leading it next. Galloway continued to pour out his experience as he admonished pastors to lead their congregations in touching all four of the essential bases: what, why, how, and when.

What Do We Need to Change?

Dale Galloway says that emphasizing what God calls a church to become and achieve must be sown as seeds of change. In casting that vision, the leader has to decide which of the following shifts that congregation most needs to make.

- From maintenance to mission
- From death to life

- From the past to the future
- From being ingrown to being outgrown
- From surviving to thriving
- From complacency to urgency
- From no growth to abundant growth

A positive basis for change comes as a result of evaluating these critical areas and establishing biblical-based core values. In the world-renowned book, *The One Minute Manager*, Ken Blanchard says, "The thinking that got you to where you are today will not take you to where you need to be tomorrow." As one continues prayerfully pinpointing the right "what" question, evaluation of the church's condition continues as well.

Why Should We Change?

Galloway further states that throughout the change process, the leader must give people a recurring answer to the "why" question. To lead people through the emotional experience of change, explain what happens if the church does not change and what happens if it does. A good formula for this is, If we do not do this, then such-and-such a serious consequence will occur. Unless people see a need for change, they will not budge. They will say, "Why do we need to change? I like things the way they are." Leaders must be proactive. They need to guard against the pull of gravity. They know that coasting can only take them downhill. If churches continue coasting, they die. Challenge your people to "greater things than these" (John 14:12). Help them get a sense of the benefits that will happen because of the change.

How Do We Frame the Change?

The "how" concept can be summarized with four Ps: **P**urpose it, **P**icture it, **P**lan it, and **P**lay it out, giving everyone a piece. Arrange all the needed changes according to priority. The leader must think through the process needed to implement the change or changes successfully. Another way to promote effective change is to develop two tracks for the church to run on simultaneously—the "old" or existing design and the newer one. You can effectively bring change if you leave everything in place. Over time, the new track may become so popular that the older track fades away without a great sense of congregational disappointment.

When Do We Make the Change?

Timing is everything. There are at least ten timing situations a leader should consider before launching a change. When you have

1. taken the time to listen to and hear from the Lord.
2. developed and earned a trust relationship with your people.
3. cultivated a strong sense among the most influential leaders that the church needs to change.
4. underscored a corporate dissatisfaction with things as they are.
5. accumulated "pocket change" (helpful recommendations) from doing some previous things well.
6. caught and built momentum. (When you have gotten the "Big Mo" you can make changes you cannot do at other times.)
7. framed a sense of urgency.
8. the confidence to say that the situation demands action right now.
9. built a high level of commitment to the needed change.
10. helped the people understand that the proposed changes are in their best interests.

If we wait until everything seems perfect, we'll miss the incredible opportunity. Bright futures do occur when we take risks. We have everything to gain from the right change and nothing to lose. Galloway quotes his life motto, which came from Robert Schuller: "I'd rather attempt something great for God and fail than do nothing and succeed." We serve a God who specializes in doing the impossible. Conrad Hilton advised, "If you want to launch big ships, go to where the water is deep." Dream big and then lead your congregation to be all God calls it to be.[38]

In 2005 at the Beeson Institute for Advanced Church Leadership, Galloway spoke on "Becoming a Successful Change Agent." He outlined the following eleven principles for effectively leading one's church through the transition of change:[39]

#1 Cast and re-cast the vision.

#2 Create a "change" leadership team.

#3 Share the vision and strategy for change with your staff.

#4 Prepare the people for change.

#5 Affirm the past.

#6 You have to communicate and communicate with clarity the purpose.

#7 Overcome complacency with urgency.

#8 Be responsive to leading the people through the adjustment zone of transition.

#9 Love people through the change.

#10 Celebrate the victories.

#11 Stick with the change until it becomes a permanent reality.

Changes in Today's Churches

This section reveals some very keen and insightful looks at the state of the church both now and in the future. This section should confirm in the heart of every spiritual leader and pastor the truthfulness of one's journey of faith in the church. Prepare to be amazed at the accuracy in stating the past practices of the church and what will become future practices:

Bill Easum, in a presentation entitled, "Transition Issues in Spiritual Redwood Churches," uses several metaphors to describe transitions that are taking place in today's churches. He lists nine transitions to look for in what he calls "Giant Redwood" churches. The first one he uses is from understanding the organization as a machine to seeing it as organic. Easum believes that this is the most notable shift of our time. Churches and denominations are living systems. They make decisions and behave differently to the same stimuli. They have a will and can choose to create something to happen. However, during most of the 20th century, church leaders tried to manage the church and their denominations as if they were inanimate passive things without a will or life force of their own.[40]

The first change we see today is a move from an institutional view of mission to seeing mission as spiritual:

1. *The Institutional Life Metaphor* concerns itself with funding church programs, doing church and denominational work, balancing the budget, and keeping buildings clean. Faith in this model of ministry is rarely seen as a life-and-death issue. *This analogy was evident in Greater Shiloh in that we used to put a lot of emphasis on administration, credentials, denominationalism, meetings, and defending the faith.*

2. *The Spiritual Life Metaphor* concerns itself with carrying out the task at all costs and living out the DNA (core beliefs) in all that it does. In this metaphor, healthy churches are not concerned with the continuity of programming or with protecting a tradition that no longer carries out the DNA. There is willingness to discontinue ministries that do not carry out the DNA. *At Greater Shiloh we used to be organized under the Missionary Society paradigm as the organizational structure for how we conducted*

mission work. We created a duel track that created the old paradigm and a new track that featured evangelism and outreach. We have now discontinued most of the old Missionary Society auxiliaries because they do not fit our new DNA.

The second change in today's churches is a move from an emphasis on the institutional church to contributing to the kingdom:

3. The Kingdom Model thinks in terms of effecting a change in or reaching an area instead of starting a church. Disciple making does not center on growing a church but in helping people to enter the kingdom. The church model emphasizes place, tradition, operations, internal affairs, competition, conceit, and acting locally. In this model, it is rare for a denomination to put a new church in an area where all of the churches of that denomination are dying. That would be too much competition to the individual churches. The Kingdom Model emphasizes territory, strategies, opportunities, outward alliances and cooperation, humility, and acting locally while thinking globally.[41] *This is primary a major shift in our ministry today at Greater Shiloh. We have developed and are developing more of a kingdom or global mindset as opposed to just the church model. We now see ourselves as agents of God, reaching and transforming the world for Christ.*

The third change in today's churches is a move from a committee understanding of *delegation* to a team understanding of *empowerment*:

4. ***The Committee Life Metaphor*** believes that laity is empowered when they "run" the church. Going to meetings and making decisions are the roles of empowerment. Getting laity to do what the institution needs done is the role of leadership. Feeding the machine takes precedence over feeding God's sheep. Activity

and involvement in the machinery is the mission, not living in the world. In such a model, control of what people do is the key. This clearly was the problem at the inception of when I became engaged in the ministry and leadership of Greater Shiloh; the emphasis was more focused on who did what rather than what we did.

5. ***The Team Life Metaphor*** believes that laity is empowered only when they are equipped to serve others. Laity is encouraged to follow their gifts not the organizational needs of the institution. Autonomous teams carry out the mission of the church without interference from the top. In this model, accountability is more important than control. *This metaphor is more of what you will find today at Greater Shiloh. People are empowered to serve in areas of ministry based upon their spiritual gifts or S.H.A.P.E. [an acronym for Spiritual Gifts, Heart, Ability, Personality, Experiences] as opposed to the pastor or leadership dictating to people what the administration needs or wants the congregation to do.*

A fourth change is that entitled church members now live as servants of Jesus Christ:

6. ***The Entitled Life Metaphor*** of leadership believes pastors are "hired guns" brought in by the church to do the ministry of the church for the laity. "Pastor Fetch" is a key role of the clergy, meaning whatever the laity needs them to do, pastors are supposed to do.

7. ***The Servant Life Metaphor*** of leadership believes that every Christian is a minister (which means a servant) because of their spiritual gifts. Spiritual gifts of selfless service are given to each

person at the point of salvation. *At Greater Shiloh we help members develop a profile of their S.H.A.P.E. The members then choose where they believe God has gifted them to serve, not as a mandate from anyone in leadership.*

8. ***The European Life Metaphor*** of education is being replaced by the *Indigenous Life Metaphor.* The early settlers of North America established European systems that were based on a Germanic education, which emphasized intellect, authoritarian posture, and distrust of the laity. Reality was processed through the head to the heart.

9. ***The Indigenous Life Metaphor*** requires church leaders to reach unchurched people through the heart, not the head. We are to develop teams and engage in collaboration. Credentials are not viewed to be as valuable as holiness. Today, we want to mobilize the laity. The three main traits of successful local church ministries are emotion, immediacy, and trust. Reality is processed now more through the heart than through the head. In the industrial world, the best way to reach people was through the head to the heart. Today, the best way to reach people is through the heart to the head. *At Greater Shiloh, we don't have it all together, but the emphasis over the past five years has been to reach unchurched people by exposing each person's need of a Savior rather than having people believe that church people are the ones who know and everybody else better get right.*

Today, the fact that we are on the mission field with Jesus is now more urgent than whether or not we have accepted theology. The church exists to be salt, light, and leaven to the world. The goal is not to grow churches but to infect the city.[42]

Implications of these shifts on worship:

We are witnessing the end of routine forms of worship. Over the next few years, we will see more and more unusual forms of congregations that will surface and with them, newer forms of worship.

Congregations will be more missional outposts than formal institutions. Worship will take on a much more informal structure, much like what is happening now in the house church movement, rather than a formal sanctuary.

Communion will be done in homes more and by laity. Remember the Passover? It was held in the home. Baptisms will become more and more adult and less ritualized, and will be carried out by laity.

We will observe the end of order and the rise of Spirit-led congregations where ecstasy and dynamic experience with God replaces order and reverence. The day of doing this, and then doing this, and then doing this, is over. The church will take on the flavor of the congregations in the book of Acts.

We will dismiss the idea of seeker-versus-believer worship. This includes seeker-driven and seeker-sensitive efforts. Neither is biblical and will be discarded as we move farther into the postmodern world. We will soon discover that it will be more like the first century than the twenty-first century. In the first century the line between the believer and the nonbeliever was not clearly drawn, neither were the lines between Jew and Christian. In the first few decades of Christianity, Christians were called Nazarenes because they were considered to be one of the many sects within Judaism such as Sadducees, Pharisees, Zealots, and others.

Jewish Christians worshiped in the temple and studied in the synagogues and kept the dietary laws. As far as first-century Christians were concerned, they were simply a new division of Judaism. Christian and Jew alike worshiped together with little thought at first of difference. We are entering that time once again. So what should we do? We should worship together, seeker and Christian. Remember, postmoderns have to belong before they believe.[43]

Spiritual issues and the transformation of adults will be the primary focus of worship. Programs and children and youth will not be the primary focus in the new world. Spiritual growth will eclipse programming and adults will get the lion's share of disciple making. Adults who have been exposed to disciple making will disciple their children, not the church. The church will still have lovely children's and youth ministries, but they will not be the focus as they have been the last thirty years.

Spiritual issues will be more valuable than style. Assisting people to experience God will replace providing an orderly flow of worship. An emphasis on life experience will replace the passion for the liturgical calendar. Adult baptism will largely replace infant baptism even in those denominations where infant baptism was the predominant form. Easum provides two reasons for predicting this change:

During Christendom, one way to distinguish churches was by how they baptized. Some practiced infant baptism and some adult baptism. Both forms served the basic mission of the church as it made disciples until recently. With the death of Christendom, more and more people are growing up outside of Christendom and, therefore, fewer and fewer people are candidates for infant baptism. People have to bring their babies to the church to be baptized. Today, those who do not grow up in the church are much less likely to come to church for anything; we must go to them. During Christendom, 85 percent of the baptisms took place before the age of 18. After the death of Christendom, 85 percent of all baptisms are likely to be adult baptisms. The practice of infant baptism is becoming more and more irrelevant in the Western world.[44]

More and more people want to experience baptism as adults, so they are asking to be re-baptized, which is a no-no in many denominations that place orthodox theology above the importance of the human experience.

Musicians will be forced to determine which is more beneficial to them: to teach people to understand quality music or to teach any music that transforms people. In most cases, they will not have a choice.

Preaching will focus on an invitation to God's grace. In other words, the service moves toward a climax, which is a response from individuals in the congregation. The service is designed to help people give their lives to Jesus Christ who can and will save all who surrender their hearts to Him.

PART III

An Approach to Change

Methodology

When God changes a church, in order to reach the un-churched, He often inspires new initiatives that will require faith. After the death of Rev. Allen Thomas, Greater Shiloh's fourth pastor, I began to lead the congregation as the fifth pastor. An earlier section of this book has already provided the circumstances through which that relationship began. But once at the helm, I asked myself and God what should I do? After much trial and error, following suit of the programmatic features of the church's storied past, God laid on my heart the desire to seek new paradigms.

The dominant intervention was developing a strategic focus and a planning process to address and improve all aspects of church life. The Kingdom Principles Growth Strategies program led us into and through this new territory. Success in life is not determined by our intentions but our decisions. Intentions must never be confused with decisions. Decisions move us from philosophy, vision, and purpose to practical actions. Planning and decision making take nothing away from God's leading a church to fulfill its divinely assigned task.

In an article titled, "Is Strategic Planning Biblical?" Mark Marshall asks, "Do we have a biblical foundation for the concept of strategic planning, or is it something we have taken from the secular business model and applied to our churches? God does honor the process of strategic planning, doesn't

He? By principle and example, God's Word establishes strategic planning as one of the ways He works in and through His people."

There are a number of leaders in Scripture who thought and acted strategically:

Moses was obviously a strategic thinker—or at least he learned to be. Soon after he led the nation of Israel out of Egypt, Moses was struggling as a leader. His father-in-law, Jethro, came to see him after hearing the incredible things God had been doing. Jethro observed that Moses was overwhelmed with the burdens of leadership and shared with him a God-given plan—a strategy—for dealing with the issue. Jethro taught Moses how to set up a strategic plan by delegating the work so that the load would be spread among many. As a result, the God-given resources were used more effectively, and the ministry was accomplished. Moses was also thinking strategically when he sent spies to the land of Canaan.

Joshua, as Moses' protégé, also demonstrated strategic leadership. In Joshua 6, God gave him a little lesson on strategic thinking. As Joshua led the Israelites into the Promised Land, they faced their first enemy. They happened to be hidden in the strong city of Jericho. God gave Joshua a strategy. He could have simply reached down from heaven and zapped the city, but God chose to work through a strategy that involved His people. God continues to work through His people today.

Nehemiah was a God-appointed leader who used a strategy. When God laid it on his heart to rebuild the walls of Jerusalem, Nehemiah began to develop and then work through a well-planned strategy to accomplish the vision God had given. He assessed the damage, secured the resources, and established leaders with specific assignments. Anyone who has ever built a structure, from a doghouse to a three-bedroom house, will acknowledge Nehemiah's need for some kind of drawn-out plan for the reconstruction of the walls of ancient Jerusalem.

David was a strategic thinker from boyhood. He did not defeat Goliath with his might or strong armor. He defeated Goliath using a God-given strategy that pinpointed the weakness of his enemy. Later, as a leader of soldiers, David used strategy in battle. David needed men who could think and plan strategically, and God gave him the men of Issachar (1 Chronicles 12:32).

We can point to **Jesus Christ** as a great example of one who had a strategy. He began by recruiting His leadership, developing them, then deploying them "to the ends of the earth" (Acts 1:8, NIV). His strategy included some public teaching and miracle working. Ultimately, Jesus' strategy took Him all the way to the Cross, the grave, and the Resurrection. Jesus Christ knew the plan to provide redemption for all of mankind long before leaving heaven. He came to carry it through.

Paul was a key player in establishing the early church; he had a strategy. It is obvious in reading the accounts of his missionary journeys that Paul chose key cities in which to establish beachheads for ministry. He chose cities where he might have the greatest influence on the largest number of people. Ephesus, for example, was the gateway to Asia Minor.

Proverbs 19:21 reads, "Many are the plans in a man's heart, but it is the Lord's purpose that prevails." God's purpose is the essential element in strategic planning for the church that is vastly different from the secular strategic planning models. We see setting our hearts and minds on God as the beginning of the strategic planning process. Without question, it is God's plan we want, not our own.

God obviously expects us to plan. He has given to us a number of clear principles along with some great examples. He makes it clear that we are not to trust our own plans and strategies and ignore the guidance of the Holy Spirit. It is only after we seek the heart of God and His direction that we can establish plans that please Him and plans that will succeed.

Strategic planning is not only a biblical concept, it is a biblical mandate. It is God's chosen method of working to establish how you and your church intend to carry out the Great Commission. Be intentional in connecting with God's heart and knowing how you will accomplish His mission in your setting.

The book of Proverbs has a number of clear, practical principles regarding strategy and planning, including Proverbs 14:15: "A simple man believes anything, but a prudent man gives thought to his steps."

- Proverbs 15:22: "Plans fail for lack of counsel, but with many advisers they succeed."

- Proverbs 16:3: "Commit to the Lord whatever you do, and your plans will succeed."

- Proverbs 16:9: "In his heart a man plans his course, but the LORD determines his steps."

- Proverbs 20:18: "Make plans by seeking advice; if you wage war, obtain guidance."

Greater Shiloh's intervention followed a six-week Bible study for 25 church leaders held from January to March 2000. I assumed the role of project director. The planning principles learned during this research continue to this day. The initial process and its annual updates have served as the basis for this research.

The growth strategies provided a guide that has allowed our church leaders to articulate our philosophy of ministry, purpose of ministry, and vision of ministry, and to coordinate all ministry strategies for the church. Each year since 2000, Greater Shiloh has used these strategies as tools in an ongoing process of evaluating the church's ministry priorities. As a result, we have avoided the traditional programmatic approach to planning and have customized plans that are unique to us. We have transitioned from philosophy about the church to good decision making for the church.

This ministry intervention has led to the rediscovery of God's plan for His church. It has provided church leaders with a clear picture of the church's strengths and composite giftedness. This gives the church assistance with future staff selection and helps leaders place members in ministry positions. In addition, we are more effectively purchasing resources, thereby making church budget a more purposeful priority.

Dr. Gene Mims states in the book, *Kingdom Principles for Church Growth*, that one of the greatest dangers we face today in church growth is making methods supreme. "Before we can implement methods, we must understand the process God uses to redeem the world through the witness of the church."[45] He cautions that we must not be so preoccupied with the search for the right method to reach an exploding population of lost people that we forget that an understanding of God's principles for kingdom growth is primary.

Mims points out that church growth is born and nourished through a process given by God Himself. Scripture reveals God consistently doing two things: creating and redeeming. God chose to create humanity in His image and to have fellowship with His created order. He further desires for us to have fellowship with one another. God chose to create every person with a will by which he or she accepts or rejects Him. In spite of our sin, God chooses to redeem a people for Himself out of the world. Redemption restores the benefits lost in the fall and provides the redeemed with fellowship with God and one another.

When Christ came to Earth, He brought salvation to persons who were in sin and separated from God. He came preaching the Good News of the kingdom and urging people to repent of their sins and to trust in Him.

Dr. Mims is convinced that the growth in God's kingdom holds the key to church growth. His book introduces and often repeats the 1-5-4 Principle of Growth.[46]

The principle involves

One (1) Driving force for church growth: The Great Commission.

Five (5) Essential church functions for church growth: Evangelism, Discipleship, Ministry, Fellowship, and Worship.

Four (4) Results: Numerical Growth, Spiritual Growth, Ministries Expansion, and Missions Advance.

He explains how each part of the principle fits the whole concept of church growth. In summary, he has identified seven kingdom principles:

Principle 1 – The church must experience God and seek His Kingdom; listen to God and then make decisions.

Principle 2 – The kingdom of God is growing, and nothing can stop it.

Principle 3 – God invites the church to join Him in His work of redemption.

Principle 4 – The Great Commission is the driving force for the church.

Principle 5 – The Bible clearly identifies five functions of the church: evangelism, discipleship, ministry, fellowship, and worship.

Principle 6 – Church growth methods follow God's process of kingdom growth.

Principle 7 – Church growth is God's supernatural work in a local church.

The Strategic Process

When God changed the direction and understanding of this church, He used the impetus of supplementary materials called *Kingdom Principles Growth Strategies: A Leader's Guide,* written by Gene Mims and Michael Miller, to serve as the implementation support for Kingdom Principles for Church Growth.[47]

The guide provided a road map for our leadership team to work our way through the growth strategy process. It provided a number of reproducible analysis grids that helped the team determine our growth priorities. The team and I prayed and sought God before each session for methodology and an understanding needed to stimulate and begin a relevant ministry to support today's churchgoers. We also prayed to fulfill the will of God for our lives and for guidance to set in order this church in a state of sustained growth.

Section I—Strategic View

I initially met quarterly with the leadership team to work through the growth strategies chart, section by section.[48] The first task was to revisit our research on the Great Commission and other Bible passages, to help determine what God is doing in the world, and what He wants to do in our church.

We then developed a purpose statement that we called our mission statement. It was a statement that would say what we were trying to accomplish. A mission statement should always reach beyond what you are able to accomplish. It is the ongoing reason why you exist as a church and what you are always trying to accomplish. In our process, our mission statement became a restatement of the Great Commission in modern terms. Team members wrote a mission statement of their own. We compared each of them and chose the best one. Collectively we revised it until satisfied that it captured the essence of what we believed God wanted Greater Shiloh to do.

Some years later I heard of Rick Warren, pastor of Saddleback Church in California, who was doing a similar work. I discovered that Rick Warren also strongly advocated mission statement development, which he positions as critical to building a healthy, strong, and growing church.[49] Not only does he say that everyone needs to know why the church exists (core values), but also what we are to be doing (mission).

Warren[50]	Malphurs[51]
Purpose Statement	Mission Statement
Biblical	Biblical
Specific (simple and clear)	A Statement (clear, articulate)
Transferable (Short enough to be remembered and passed on to everybody in the church.)	Brief
Measurable	Broad

Mission Statement

The mission of Greater Shiloh Baptist Church is to reach, teach, and baptize throughout the world, beginning in our community, fulfilling the Great Commission by the power and presence of the Holy Spirit until Jesus returns.

The leadership team then developed a vision statement. A vision statement defines how the church intends to fulfill its role. The vision statement portrays a future state of the church, the direction the congregation will take to achieve its goal and fulfill the Great Commission. We now use both statements on all printed material and recite them periodically in worship services. We teach them in the new member classes to ensure that all members know and understand the purpose and vision of our church.[52]

Vision Statement

We will fulfill this mission through evangelism, discipleship, ministry, fellowship, and worship. The results will be spiritual, numeric, ministry, and mission growth.

Discover the Church's Spiritual Gifts

The next step in the strategic process required that the leadership team determine each church member's spiritual gifts and develop a composite of the church's spiritual giftedness. The pastor's spiritual gifts were also included in this. A ministry gifts inventory was provided to all active members of the church over a three-week period. Each member was asked to complete a gift inventory and leave it in designated foyer and lobby areas of the church building. The team collected and scored composites, which determined the church's spiritual gifts. A separate composite revealed the pastor's spiritual gifts.

This process then allowed us to compare the spiritual gifts of the pastor and leaders to those of the rest of the church family. This process revealed similarities and differences between the giftedness of the pastor and the other members of the congregation. The results revealed the church's strengths for ministry.

My personal ministry gifts inventory analysis revealed strengths in the areas of teaching, mercy, leadership, and exhortation.[53] The Greater Shiloh Church Giftedness Composite list revealed strengths in giving, helps, administration, and mercy.[54] This information provided at least the following benefits for us: (1) We have developed a report on each member and his or her gifts, abilities, and possibilities for use. (2) The composite provided us a guide to minister according to strengths.

The leadership team was assigned the task of defining Greater Shiloh Church's Strengths, Weaknesses, Opportunities, and Threats (SWOTS).[55] The project director led a brainstorming activity in each of the above areas. Responses were recorded from team members and placed in Strategic Process Grids.[56]

SWOTS

Strengths	Weaknesses	Opportunities	Threats
Pastor— teaching, preaching, administration, spiritual gifts	Missing spiritual gifts of prophecy, shepherding and evangelism	Evangelize West End community; Improve fellowship; Develop missions	Tradition Cliques Selfishness Complacency
Congregation— giving, helping, and mercy spiritual gifts	Lack of commitment to core ministry; Lack of awareness among congregation	Launch new ministries; Improve and expand worship	Lack of devotion to God; Lack of unity in the church
Membership— lots of men, young families, and a strong financial base	Not enough properly functioning auxiliaries; Inconsistent, therefore ineffective, deacon family ministry	Expand teaching to reach all; Create children's church	Lack of proper preparation; Ignorance in not knowing; Unwillingness to learn
Ministries— Christian Ed., Bible classes, Music, Deaconess, Mission, Youth, Usher, Elderly, Athletic, Radio, Tape/Video, Internet and Intercessory Prayer	Too many separate agendas Unwillingness to support Pastor's vision; Weak and insincere fellowship	Revamp auxiliaries and organizations for effectiveness Utilize more technology	Unwillingness to trust one another Improper staffing

Map Section IIa.—Possibility Grids

During the Bible study from the book, *Kingdom Principles for Church Growth*, we identified five church functions (evangelism, discipleship, ministry, fellowship, worship) that enable the church to fulfill the Great Commission like a kingdom church. These functions follow the progress of a person from salvation through spiritual growth to service. Our church included these functions in our vision statement because they certainly do explain how we intend to accomplish our mission and purpose.

During this strategic process, the leadership team and I did an analysis of our church as it relates to each of the five functions. We prepared a matrix for each function.[57] A grid was prepared on evangelism, one for discipleship, ministry, fellowship, and worship. In each grid, we listed as many events, programs, and ministries that represented present church activities, possibilities of what it could do, and a picture of what it would like to do. This project helped church leaders clearly link the association of the Great Commission to the five essential church functions, the four results, and the biblical process.

We were able to make observations, evaluations, and some decisions about our church's ministry. We ranked the items from each grid in order of importance from highest priority to lowest. It was not difficult to determine the priorities at either spectrum, whether highest or lowest. The difficulty was deciding the order of items that were similar. At that time, a total of sixty-two identified activities were placed in twenty-nine grids[58] which represented the possibilities that our church had to fulfill if we were going to accomplish its newly stated mission, vision, and the Great Commission.

Map Section IIb.—Ministry Resource Analysis

There are five different analyses that were applied to the resources that we identified as necessary to achieve the mission and vision of the church.

The analysis included the number of time-related resources, space resources, people resources, financial resources, and training resources. Each analysis revealed needs, strengths, and potential of the ministry activities listed in the grids.

Time-related Resources

Every activity in a church requires time and people. People have a limited number of hours to spend attending and serving in a church. We estimated that the average church member spends about three hours per week in church. When we considered our priority list from the possibility grids, we discovered that the first three items listed would require almost all of the hours available.

We listed Sunday morning worship, Sunday school, and midweek Bible study as our top three priorities. Each of those would require at least one hour each. The hourly totals for each of the sixty-two strategic activities had to be assessed. Some ministry activities occur weekly, some monthly, and some annually. We were able to work out a different schedule for activities that occurred on an irregular basis.

Space Resources

The objective was to determine whether our church had space available for the activities we wanted to plan. Designated space is a must for every activity our church or any church conducts. We drew two diagrams: one of the church's facilities, the other for each day of the week. We attempted to place each activity in a room. It confirmed what we already knew. The space at that location was inadequate for some of the current and planned future activities.

People Resources

The analysis of ministry personnel provided an excellent opportunity for me as project director to raise awareness among church leaders. We needed to move away from friendship appointments toward placing people in the right place for the right reasons. That would require greater consideration and use of a person's spiritual gifts and abilities when matching current and future ministry positions.

Financial Resources

Every activity in a local church requires financial resources. I have always been a man of faith, believing that where God guides, God provides. Analyzing financial needs and resources helps the church evaluate ministry activities on the basis of cost to anticipated value and ministry impact. We concluded that our church had to begin to build its annual budget plan based on priorities of the ministry, not on past assumptions with a few adjustments here and there. We determined that it was essential to know the costs of each activity and the need to remind the congregation of its financial responsibility to the Lord.

Training Resources

The issue of training was identified as critical for the sustained future success of our church. Every activity required a certain level of competency and skill. We identified several areas where training was needed. Other areas were projected for future development. Leadership growth opportunities for all church leaders were viewed as an immediate need. We noted that one entire area was missing: evangelism. Hence, evangelism training was also listed as an immediate need.

Map Section IIc.—Expected Changes/Results

Often our leadership team reviewed and remembered that when we practiced the five functions adopted in our Vision Statement (evangelism, discipleship, fellowship, ministry, and worship) as they should be, we could expect or impact four consistent results: numerical growth, spiritual growth, ministry growth, and missions advance. These represent changes in a congregation and its members' lives. Strategic planning assumes changes will occur.

Our aim was that the changes would be beneficial. Changes or results should be considered in two categories: hard changes, which can be quantified and measured numerically in increases or decreases; and soft changes, which cannot be measured numerically but are relevant.

We probed each represented ministry on the team, until we had a thorough understanding of programs, products, and services that were to be offered in the upcoming church year. We produced a schedule of planned activities. Based on that calendar of events, we made a list of expected changes that were to occur by quarters during the following church year.[59] We considered four areas that could be measured by attendance: worship service, Bible study, discipleship events, and new ministry development.

Greater Shiloh Missionary Baptist Church operates its church year based on a fiscal calendar year that runs from October 1 through September 30. Our first quarter-end is December, the second is March, the third is June, and the fourth is September.

Soft changes are changes in spiritual growth, perceptions, feelings, moods, and attitudes. These results would include changes in lost persons' attitudes toward the church, a growing spirit of love and fellowship in the congregation, and a spirit of celebration and praise in worship. With respect to soft changes, the leadership team decided that we would develop a greater sense of family among church members. We wanted to create a priority of developing an intentional spirit of love, fellowship, a spirit of celebration and praise in worship. We also noted needed changes in spiritual perceptions, feelings, moods, and poor attitudes. To evaluate the soft changes, we developed a churchwide survey to allow members of the congregation to respond to various areas of church life.[60]

Map Section III—Actions

The biblical growth strategy process is the way a church grows people and incorporates them into its family. Every church functions according to a ministry system whether it realizes it or not. Greater Shiloh's method was weak and unclear. We did not have an assimilation process. We were guilty of allowing people to unite with the fellowship and in many cases move them directly into a ministry auxiliary or even a leadership position. People were often undeveloped in their understanding of God and lacked biblical understanding. When difficulties or challenges confronted them, often they would not have what they needed to stand. We did change that process. We began with a basic new member orientation course.

However, since that time we have experimented with different assimilation processes and have adopted a version that has made a tremendous difference. We now use a model adapted from Rick Warren's work at Saddleback Church called C.L.A.S.S., extensive, long-term core classes adapted for church members. We began by introducing people to the Word of God, either in worship or through a Bible study. We seek to engage lost people through both. Inspired people go through a series of discipleship classes:

Class 101: Discovering Church Membership offers to help persons examine what it means to be committed to Christ and then to the local church family. The course covers the basis of our Christian faith and provides an understanding of why we exist as a church. It covers our strategy of describing those we are trying to reach, and tells the internal structure of the church and our affiliations.

Class 201: Introduction to Spiritual Maturity assists persons in growing toward spiritual maturity by exposing them to four habits that every Christian needs in order to become like Christ.

Class 301: Introduction to Your SHAPE helps persons discover their unique design for using their God-given gifts and abilities in serving God and others in the local church. (SHAPE is an acronym for a blend of spiritual gifts: Service, Heart, Ability, Personality and Experience.)

Class 401: Discovering My Life Mission prepares for equipping and empowering committed Christians for the world and life-changing missions. All class participants sign a required commitment card at the conclusion of each class.

Class 501: Discovering Stewardship is an additional class that Greater Shiloh developed to help persons discover that God is owner of everything and we are managers of what He has entrusted to us. We are managers of our time, talents, and treasures and as such should use them for God's glory and His purposes on earth.

Map Section IV—Evaluation

In order for strategic processes of thinking to be of maximum value to the church, all strategic plans and efforts toward fulfilling those plans must be evaluated periodically. Some of them are evaluated weekly, monthly, quarterly, and annually. We have increased the frequency of meetings with different segments of leaders to evaluate our church's progress toward expected changes.

Administrative staff meetings, held each week, included office staff and program directors that informed and reported on all current and future ministry plans and issues. Deacons connected monthly in accountability and training meetings designed to discuss ministry concerns of church members and to receive updates on the status of church affairs. Quarterly meetings called SALT—Shiloh Advanced Leadership Training—are held to provide leadership tips and other information regarding policy, operations, and the calendar of events to church leaders. Two semi-annual leadership conferences are held with all church leaders. One meeting is held in the spring of the year (usually in May) to look at any needed mid-course corrections and another leadership conference, held in August, to plan for the upcoming church year.

The entire congregation participates in a strategic annual business conference designed to assess progress of all ministry efforts and forecast projections for each new church year. An annual update of the Greater Shiloh Missionary Baptist Church Ministry Plan has provided continual guidelines for this church and has charted a course of outward mobility.

This strategic planning process was the beginning. It has put this pastor and church on a path that has led to tremendous growth. In each subsequent year since 2000, we have updated the annual strategic plan.[61] This process has taken the guess work out of what we are to be doing. We have continually prayed and studied successful church-wide campaigns and models from some of America's leading churches. We have adopted some of those models and customized them to fit our specific needs.

We have grown by leaps and bounds just as the four results promised:

Spiritually—Members are maturing regularly, rapidly.

Numerically—We have grown from less than 300 to nearly 3,000 members.

Ministries expanded—We have developed more than fifty ministries led by lay leaders.

Missions advanced—We have advanced from a few mission meetings to large community venues where thousands of people are fed with food and clothing. We are mobilizing hundreds of volunteers for local mission action projects and are now poised for global mobilization.

PART IV

A Change Has Come

Discussion of Transitions at Greater Shiloh

This section examines the actual transitions we have made and applies the truths of the research and the research project to demonstrate that it is possible for God to change a church and guide it toward regaining its missionary call.

God has changed Greater Shiloh Missionary Baptist Church in an amazing way. From its humble beginnings through its former days of glory, God has been at work. The transitions described are those that have taken place more recently. In reality, there are eight specific transitions that this church has already made, with more under way.

Goal

We set out to find ways to cause the congregation to regain its outward, missionary focus. Having experienced a period of decline, the emphasis was on survival—maintaining the status quo. Most people did not even realize that the church had slipped into such a low state, because it happened in the regular life cycle of the church. There was no major announcement that affirmed that the church was in a period of decline. Even for me, coming in as a young minister, I did not fully understand all of the dynamics at play. However, it was quite clear that a change had to take place.

A transition was set in motion when the church's long-term leader and fourth pastor, Rev. Allen Thomas, acknowledged a need for an assistant. The transition began when I arrived to assist him. The need for more transition became apparent when he passed. We have successfully transitioned from an internally focused church that was in maintenance mode, to an outwardly focused church, now particularly concerned for others, the lost, the disadvantaged, as well as those at the other end of the spectrum who also need God. Whenever we look into the Word of God, we discover God's mandates and God's design. The spiritual journey into strategic inquiry was what God used to come on board and steady a wayward ship that had lost its captain, to train the new captain to understand the navigational instruments, and to chart a new course for the ship.

Approach

Our approach to ministry has transitioned away from being program- and personality-driven, centering on having a large number of Sunday afternoon programs called annual days. The church depended on those annual days to give itself identity and presence. Annual days were used to drive finances or raise money, as congregants were asked for specific amounts to contribute for each occasion. Days like Men's Day, Women's Day, or Choir Anniversary or any number of such designations drove the church.

Personalities also were prominent in the approach used to direct the church. Whenever a charming or a warm personality is in charge, people usually don't complain as much or hardly notice the personality. When a person with a not-so-pleasing personality is among the key leaders, personality stands out as being dominant in how that church functions. Greater Shiloh has had its share of both types of personalities that helped guide the church in one direction or another. However, we have now transitioned to a purpose-driven model.

Five biblical purposes of God as outlined in the Scriptures are what now drive this church. Rick Warren once said, "The church is going to look like something, and it is going to be driven by something." The issue is what or who is going to drive this church? We have resolved that we are purpose-driven by affirming it through our mission and vision statements. By changing the way we are organized, we have affirmed that our church will be led by the purposes of God as described in the Great Commandment in Matthew 22:36-40, and in the Great Commission in Matthew 28:19-20. We have also adopted the full set of purpose-driven characteristics that guide our practices.

Target

We have transitioned from reaching "fellow Baptists," that is, members of other local assemblies, to reaching the un-churched. Intentional evangelism never crossed my mind in years past. I did not see, or perhaps understand, evangelism as a biblical mandate. I used to be of the mindset that people came to church by choice. Those who came would be loved and those who chose not to come were welcome whenever they were led to do so. I did not see it as my task to go after them. Street evangelism and door-to-door evangelism did not appeal to me. It wasn't practiced in any of the Baptist churches that I had been a part of. In fact, according to William J. Abraham, in his book, *The Logic of Evangelism*, "Christianity has been a part of the fabric of the West for so long that it has been assumed that Christians do not really need to evangelize."[62]

However, the settled conviction that lost people really do matter to God, and that the local church is truly the hope of the world, has fueled a new passion in me, for people who are not a part of any church. I began to realize that people who are far apart from God would spend a hopeless eternity separated from Him, unless they were led to a saving knowledge of Him. Our church has embraced as its primary target lost people and people who have a marginal relationship with God. We have set our sights upon the vast numbers of people who are not attending any church. Those are the people we are inviting to worship with us. Our desire is to lead them to faith in Christ, and turn them into fully devoted followers of Jesus Christ. I will further clarify our target as I later describe our strategy. Evangelism has also transitioned our entire perspective of missions.

We have definitely transitioned from missions consisting of house-to-house fellowships or meetings among a few dedicated sisters. We have transitioned from the Missionary Society as the basis of the church's mission program, to a more defined local and global missions focus. We are much more intentional as we mobilize our members to engage in missions work beyond the walls of the church building. We regularly mobilize teams to visit local nursing homes, providing personal care for those bereft of families. We send regular volunteers to local shelters, and participate in meal preparation and distribution in the kitchens of those shelters. In addition, monthly, we visit parks downtown where we provide lunch for homeless persons. We have launched a prison ministry that seeks to provide spiritual and donation support to male and female inmates, and in the local city and county jails as well as the state and federal prisons. We have incorporated our youth in the outreach process as several have served on mission teams to nearby states. Some of our associate ministers have gone to New York and Vermont to assist with some church planting activities in these areas.

We have touched international communities largely by sending the senior pastor—me—as a missionary to share the Gospel in China, parts of Europe, West Africa, Israel, and India. Recently, others have served in Ethiopia. We have provided food and clothing items to the poor and to orphans in Africa. And lastly, we have responded to world-relief efforts in places challenged by natural disasters, such as Haiti. Our latest efforts are aimed at changing the mindset of the church from being a church with a missions program to becoming a church whose DNA is missions.

Worship Style

We have transitioned from a strictly traditional style of worship to what I call a blended, contemporary worship style. We have altered the instrumentation of instruments and the style of music. At first, the only instrument used in the worship service was piano or organ, sometimes both. Hymns were sung using freestyle (without music, known in African-American churches as "Dr. Watts" or "long meter") and more traditional hymns with piano or organ accompaniment. We have transitioned to add other instruments: a drum set, a bass guitar, a horn section of two trumpets, an alto saxophone, and a tenor saxophone.

We still sing some of the traditional hymns, but with a lot more flair, using all of the instruments together. There is also an increase in the variety of contemporary music, some even bordering on jazz or gospel rock, thus a blend of both. Most, but not all, of old "Dr. Watts" style of hymn singing has gone. It amounts to us running a dual track, using a little bit of both styles while we are still transitioning. Deacons still maintain a limited function during the devotion for a portion of service entitled "Hymns of Our Fathers." That is followed by the employment of a praise team that usually sings contemporary songs to engage the audience in a more celebratory frame of mind as worship begins.

The use of more technology has been a major transition within our church. We have installed wireless service for computer use throughout the building. We have installed two control booths, one for audio and one for video. In the audio booth, we have installed a digital mixing board to control the quality and volume of sound during worship services. Sound quality and control can now be achieved for the choir, lead vocalist, all musical instruments, and orators. In the video booth, we have installed control panels that determine the functions of house lighting and stage theatre lighting; also added is a video switcher that controls digital video camera displays. Multiple computers loaded with worship software are used to display various media presentations on two large, mounted video screens during worship services to enhance and facilitate audience participation. High-definition video cameras record the services and compact discs and DVDs are dubbed and sold in the church bookstore. Some recordings are edited and used for television and radio broadcasts.

Gone are hymnals, as the words to songs are displayed on the screens. Scripture passages are featured on a big projection screen, so that everyone can see them together. In addition, video and movie clips, graphics, and other enhancing tools are available to support various features within a given worship service. The technology transition began while we were still worshipping in the old church, as we experimented regularly with sound mixing boards. Some limited video projections and movie clips were used during our midweek first Wednesday service. During that time, we used standup screens. Standup screens and video projections were also used for PowerPoint® presentations during seminars.

We have installed flat screen monitors in the front foyer, along the corridors, in the kitchen, bookstore, and nursery classrooms, to allow real-time viewing of the worship service. In addition, large projection screens are installed in the gym/fellowship hall, which serves as an overflow area, and in the children's chapel. Multifunctional use of these areas allows for technologically advanced presentations of information and materials, for a variety of venues such as movie nights, seminars, weddings, and funerals.

Since the first edition of this book, we have engaged in expanded public media use. Our radio, television, and Internet ministries have propelled our reach to audiences of worldwide proportions. We now have twelve radio broadcasts in ten cities across the United States of America. We have three television broadcasts on the local CBS affiliate that reaches twenty-seven counties and over one million homes in the state of Alabama. In addition, our broadcast is live-streamed over the Internet via the CBS television website. We make the weekly sermons available for listening on our church website. We distribute to thousands of subscribers worldwide a daily devotional message delivered to the mailbox of patrons five days a week and we publish a quarterly devotional inspirational book that is distributed via mail list and made available through our bookstore. Full worship service live streaming is expected to be available later this year.

Leadership

We have transitioned in our organizational structure and leadership practices from a committee/deacon board-led church to a staff-led church. We still maintain deacons but not as a *board of controls* as they once functioned. The non-biblical idea of board of controls crept into the church in the late 1800s during the rise of the democratic revolution. The rights of individuals started to be taken more serious. Business problems began to be discussed by groups in an effort to find acceptable solutions.

Often these groups met for a meal around a wooden or board table to discuss their problems. By easy transfer of meaning, the word *board* became identified with any group of persons charged with decision making. Phrases such as "board of directors" and "board of trustees" soon became a part of daily conversation. As deacons assumed much of the management of church properties and finances in the late 1800s, the business-world concept of a "board of directors" was unfortunately transferred to the church.[63]

The concept of deacons as a "deacon board" was rooted deeply in Greater Shiloh. However, through teaching the Word of God, death, attrition, and time, we have transitioned to a staff-led church. The senior pastor, paid staff, and five lay leaders (called directors) perform the administrative functions. The functions of deacons are closer to the biblical model of co-laborers with the pastor in implementing the church's function of ministry. The deacons have a family ministry where they are responsible to ministering to the needs of the families within the church. There is a limited governance function as well. There remains a plurality of leadership; a revised and updated constitution and bylaws define the roles and authority lines of church officers to flesh out who does what.

The staff-led paradigm is one of the most critical parts of the puzzle of building a great church. It is the process of creating a fine work team of church employees and volunteers, to give rise to the various parts of the vision, or master plan, of the church. The value is gained by allowing persons other than clergy and church officers to be involved in some level of decision making. The Bible teaches that "God has placed all members in the body as it has pleased Him." This allows a greater use of the spiritual gifts the Holy Spirit has given to the church. However, staff persons should be persons who are ministry-centered rather than performer-centered. Everyone on our staff has the same number-one job description: to recruit, equip, and train lay leaders in their area of ministry according to their spiritual gifts.

Conventional wisdom notes that it is essential that the senior pastor of any church have the ability to choose staff. Again, those choices should be based on ability, spiritual gifts, and trust. Our staffing plan answers the question of *whom* in our master plan. It tells who provides leadership in which areas of ministry. Currently, the organizational chart reveals the flow of responsibility and the reporting lines. The senior pastor serves as the under-shepherd, under Christ, and is the church's overseer. All ministries emanate out of the office of the pastor. Church leaders who are charged with the responsibility of leading include the deacons, trustees, ministers, and a stewardship team, which includes business affairs functions. Additional hired personnel and facilities management teams work closely with the senior pastor as input in each of these areas come directly from him.

Our administrative assistant works directly with the pastor to assist with his tasks and to relieve some of the administrative duties. In addition, the administrative assistant supervises church personnel and ensures church policies are carried out in an efficient manner. Finally, the administrative assistant works with various aspects of church leadership, but focuses mainly on the five ministry team directors to ensure that ministry plans are carried out as approved and that we maintain balance and biblical relevancy.

Each of the five ministry teams is assigned a biblical purpose according to our mission and vision statement and objectives for the church and a target audience. The Missions Team, which serves the biblical purpose of evangelism, has the target population of the community. The Maturity Team serves the biblical purpose of discipleship and has the target audience of growing believers. The Ministry Team, which serves the biblical purpose of ministry, seeks to equip the core of our membership for service. The Membership Team, which serves the biblical purpose of fellowship, seeks to care for the congregation. The Music Magnification Team, which serves the biblical purpose of worship, targets the crowd that attends weekend services.

Each of those teams is led by a lay leader, known as a director. Future plans envision the directors serving as full-time employees, and persons filling those roles would be people having that unique call on their lives to serve as pastors of those functions instead of directors.

Their primary function is to work with several sub-teams that make up the parts which deliver ministry according to their unique biblical purpose. In the new concepts of leadership within the church, we have placed a premium on developing lay leaders. Effective leaders are essential for ministry excellence. Without established mechanisms to develop leaders, growing ministries become anemic as they are left without the necessary pool of spiritually mature leaders to meet the ever-increasing ministry demands. We believe that it is an essential function of the church to define leaders, develop them, and deploy them into areas where they are passionate and gifted.

A structured leadership development program has helped to ensure that a prepared group of leaders are always available. In 2003, we secured the services of Dr. Ronald Williams from Baltimore, Maryland, to come to Birmingham to facilitate the development of a Leadership School. We put a design team together, headed by Rev. Cecelia Walker, to develop the modules and the curriculum. Our leadership program is an intensified study for persons who have completed our church member introductory C.L.A.S.S. Program.

The C.L.A.S.S. Program gives a person a proper set of spiritual underpinnings needed to ground one in the Christian faith and ensure a deepening personal walk with the Lord. That program becomes the first prerequisite for consideration as a candidate to Leadership School.

A second requirement is that members have developed profiles that indicate that at least one of their top three spiritual gifts involves administration or leadership. A member should be active in a ministry for at least one year prior to enrolling in Leadership School and have a desire to serve in a leadership capacity. Over the past ten years we have graduated more than 300 church leaders. Our curriculum features seven learning modules:

1. Quality Work
2. Accountability for the Job;
3. Handling the People with Whom We Serve;
4. Working in Teams;
5. Maintaining Spiritual Renewal;
6. The Demeanor, Behavior, and Attitude of the Leader;
7. Management of Resources and Church Policies.[64]

Ministry

We have transitioned from professional clergy doing all of the work of ministry to sharing responsibilities with lay persons. Previously, the senior pastor was expected to do all of the sick visitations, be present at every meeting, and do all of the teaching. Today, we have a shared ministry. The approach to ministry is more toward serving individuals rather than institutional.

Appropriate ministry descriptions have been developed for each area of ministry. One example would be the Deacon Family Ministry Plan. Each deacon-and-wife team is expected to fulfill a ministry role with the families assigned to them under the Deacon Family Ministry Plan. Deacons make regular calls on those families as well as assisting during times of crisis. The first line of contact for families is through their assigned deacon. Another example of how individuals are assuming roles in ministry is seen in the orientation process, as new members go through the new member program of C.L.A.S.S.

When members reach the third class in the series, Class 301, they develop their personal profile called "My SHAPE for Ministry." SHAPE is an acronym for Spiritual gifts, Heart, Abilities, Personality, and Experience. The process of identifying the specific traits that each person has in each of those areas ensures that people serve in the area of ministry according to their SHAPE. Representatives from the Ministry Team equip lay leaders and guide members by interviewing them. They then provide ministry menus of existing sub-teams with service opportunity openings. In cases where there is not a match, new ministries can be formed with that person being the point person for the new development. Sub-team leaders of the various ministries then train or equip the new person that selected their team as a matching opportunity for them.

Our leaders are provided on-going development and support through quarterly meetings called SALT (Shiloh Advanced Leadership Training). Those meetings usually consist of information sharing and using opportunities to view video clips that convey leadership tips, skills, and/or strategies. In addition, all church leaders are invited to attend two major seminars on leadership held at strategic times during the church year.

Strategy

We have transitioned from a church without a systematic method for reaching the lost, to a church with a specific strategy to reach lost people, and lead them to become fully devoted followers of Jesus Christ. We can now define very clearly our target audiences, and how we intend to move people sequentially along, until they are incorporated into the core ministry of the church. We have adopted a model similar to the one described by Rick Warren in *The Purpose-Driven Church*. We have adapted actual portions of text from that model that we now use in our C.L.A.S.S. process. Today, we have five targets, which are described and defined by using five concentric circles as shown in a visual graphic to display the targets. The visual display of circles represents the five biblical purposes defined in our mission and vision statements and the particular human audience that each purpose will address.

At the center of our church is the circle that represents the core. The core circle represents the people who are involved in participating in different lay ministries of the church. They are the leaders, the workers, and the servers. They are the Sunday school teachers, greeters, ushers, people who manage the children's ministry, youth ministry, and other youth-related activities. Getting to the core involves taking the first three of four C.L.A.S.S. membership—Classes 101, 201, and 301. When a person completes Class 301, an interview is scheduled with one of the members of the Ministry

Team. The Ministry Team has the target audience of the core, because they are responsible for identifying and equipping people to serve. The person's profile of their SHAPE developed during Class 301 is instrumental in determining the area of ministry which best suits service.

Moving from the center circle, the next circle represents the group designated as the *Committed*. These people have completed Class 201; they are those who are committed; they are growing in their faith. They believe in Christ but have not yet become active in serving the church through a ministry team. They are the prime target audience for the Maturity Team, which will seek to lead them deep into a relationship with Christ through various Bible studies, small groups, and seminars.

The next group is a bit larger and consists of the actual members of the church who have completed Class 101 and are committed to membership.

A person is not really a participating member of this church until he or she has committed to the membership requirements—one of them being taking Class 101. We call that group the congregation. They are assigned to the Membership Team, which has the biblical purpose of fellowship. The Membership Team has the responsibility of assimilating members into the family and providing care for all of the members of our local congregation. The congregation is more than persons who attend the services—they are actual members of our church.

The next circle represents a group of persons who are known as regular attendees; they are committed to attendance. This group shows up on Sunday morning. We call them the crowd. The crowd consists of believers, church members, visitors, and those who may not yet believe and they are the target audience of the Music Magnification Team, assigned the biblical purpose of worship. This team seeks to give themselves to the Lord each week so that authentically inspired worship takes place. They seek to usher in the presence of God so that all who attend worship services may have an inspirational experience.

The outer circle is called the community and is assigned to the Missions Team. The Missions Team has the biblical purpose of evangelism and outreach. The outer circle represents the un-churched people or people who marginally attend church within the community. The community consists of every person within driving distance of our church that we would like to reach for Jesus Christ. We want them to come to know Christ. Our strategy involves our members inviting their un-churched family members, friends, co-workers, neighbors, and so forth, to come out of the community and be a part of our crowd on Sundays.

We believe that our service is strong and our message is true. Scripture teaches that "faith comes by hearing, hearing the Word of God." If the un-churched or marginally churched comes within hearing distance, we believe that they will be encouraged to return again and again until convicted. Our hope is that they will unite in fellowship with us, and we can move them closer to the core.

In each of these classes, we have a covenant agreement for attendees to sign. The idea is to teach commitment in gradual steps. Each part of the process provides an opportunity to make a small commitment. When a person is asked to come out of the community and attend church, he or she makes a minimal commitment. He or she returns again and soon he or she walks the aisle, making a commitment to accept Christ as his or her Savior and request membership in His church. We seek to seal those initial commitments and gradually build others through the class covenant agreements.

The first covenant agreement takes place at the end of Class 101 and is called the Membership Covenant. In this covenant, the agreement is a commitment to Christ and the Greater Shiloh Missionary Baptist Church family. Class 101 seeks to explain what God has done for us in salvation, and explain why we exist as a church family. The Maturity Covenant, explained in Class 201, is a commitment to the habits necessary for spiritual growth. The Ministry Covenant is a commitment to discovering and using one's God-given gifts and abilities in serving God and others. The Missions Covenant is examined in Class 401 and develops the commitment to share the Good News with others. Recently, we have added Class 501, the Stewardship Covenant, which emphasizes commitment to manage God's resources of our time, talents, and treasures as God directs. Regardless of the type of commitment people select, we know that they become whatever they are committed to. The ultimate goal is to develop committed people.

Schedule

We have transitioned from a period of low visibility to one of high visibility, from a period of decline to one of upward mobility. We have transitioned from a single worship service on Sundays, to two services on Sunday and a midweek service. After the church relocated to the West End Community in 1968, there was a five-year period of enthusiasm, followed by a ten-year period characterized by decline. During the period of decline, there was one worship service, and attendance was so light that figures were not taken. The membership was dwindling; the congregation had aged with their pastor, Rev. Thomas. The church had done a dynamic work under Rev. Thomas. They had proven the impossible by managing to complete the upper level of the sanctuary of a building where worship had taken place in the basement since 1927. It was completed in 1961, only to enjoy the fruits of those labors for eight years before being forced to move. That enthusiastic congregation came to West End on fire. They purchased a facility from the defunct Temple Baptist Church. Not long after that they expanded the seating capacity and shortly thereafter, they burned the mortgage. Then came the period from 1973 to 1983; weariness was setting in and age became a factor for Pastor Thomas and many who had come with him.

December 1983 was when I was invited to preach; I was invited back again in February 1984, and offered the position of assistant pastor. After a few years, we noticed gradual increases. Attendance figures began to be recorded. Soon chairs were being put out in the aisles because the seating capacity of the sanctuary was exhausted. That prompted the study and discussion of developing a second worship service on Sunday mornings.

The new service would have an earlier start time of 8:00 a.m., while the existing 11:00 a.m. service time would remain in place. The Sunday school hour would be between the two services at 9:30 a.m. At first, both worship services were designed to mirror each other. I was afraid that the membership would prefer one service over the other. The new service started small; about ninety people attended the first one we held. However, both services have grown steadily since then. We are consistently at or near capacity now at both Sunday services. Often we have to use the overflow areas on days when seating has been exhausted.

We have had a steady stream of classes on Wednesday nights, which has traditionally been family night. There are classes for various age groups. Our incorporating a midweek service had been discussed before in strategic planning sessions without any real resolve. However, in 2003 we decided that we would launch a monthly midweek service to be held on the first Wednesday of each month. The purpose of the service was designed to be a growth engine, bringing new people to the church. We wanted to experiment with a full contemporary service, which would utilize technology, a praise band, and words on the screen, as well as video clips. We wanted to target a group that did not normally come to the church in the middle of the week. We also thought that we could attract other people from the community that would not come on Sundays. The initial testing phase of first Wednesday services was met with tremendous success.

We have now chosen to commit to maintaining the first Wednesday of the month service. As a result, we have expanded it as a growth engine, by hosting a number of multicultural ministries, preachers, community pastors, along with their congregations to share with us. Included among these offerings have been other African-American pastors and preachers; a missionary from the Philippines; young associate ministers; pastors from predominantly Caucasian congregations; and a local nondenominational Group called the Awaken Tour. All of our efforts have been to promote the Gospel, while reaching audiences that would not normally be in attendance. Future plans include the employment of more missionaries to tell their stories to strengthen our global impact efforts.

We are in agreement with what author Dan Southerland said: "Vision is not just a destination; it is a journey. Vision is not just a product; it is a process. Vision is not just the finish line; it is the whole race."[65] Greater

Shiloh is in the race for the long haul. We are committed to God, to His purposes for His church, and for our lives individually.

We have been discussing what happens when God changes a church in order to reach the un-churched. We understand that the process of transitioning the model of a church ministry from a traditional, program-driven church, to becoming a biblical purpose-driven model is a major journey. Every step requires course corrections along the way. The challenge for us has been and continues to be to learn as we go, and make the necessary changes along the way. Only a fool does not learn as he endeavors on his journey. The only thing more painful than learning from experience is not learning from experience.

Dan Southerland, who based his book, *Transitioning*, on the Scriptures as recorded in the book of Nehemiah, says that there are eight key evidences that vision has caught on. We put those evidences to the test and have applied them to our local situation and we can now affirm them as the truth. Southerland's keys and our evidence include the following:

1. *Completion of the vision.* One of the proofs that God was in Nehemiah's work was the completion of the wall. One of the proofs that God is at work in His church is the completion of the vision. A half-completed vision is not the goal. A completed transition is the goal. God did not rest until the world was completed. God does not quit working on His vision for His church until it is completed. He is a finisher.

The evidence that God is in the transition of Greater Shiloh is apparent in distinct facts: We have successfully transitioned our model of ministry into a purpose-driven church. We have completed the construction of a new facility and are poised to complete other expansions given by God's vision for this church as outlined in our five-year master plan. All portions of it will be completed this year.

2. *Obvious demonstration of God's work.* The completing of the wall had an obvious and immediate effect on all who saw it. When a God thing starts to happen in a church, even the enemies of the church know it is a God thing. It is that obvious. When a vision is working, it is obvious that God is the one at work because there is no possible explanation other than God. That is further evidence that God is at work in Greater Shiloh. There is no other explanation of what has happened and how it has happened except to say that God did it! It is so obvious that even enemies have had to acknowledge God's hand upon us. In five years, God more than tripled the size of the congregation's membership, finances, and exposure in the community, the nation, and the world. This is the work of God!

3. *Continued opposition and criticism.* Nehemiah had widespread opposition and criticism as he began his vision, and that was to be expected. He also had opposition and criticism throughout the project, and that is not surprising. Yet it is amazing to me that even when he had finished the project, which even his enemies acknowledged was done with God's help, he was still dealing with opposition and criticism. Some would think that by now the criticism would have stopped. The reality is this: it never does. The only person with no opposition is the person who is doing nothing worth opposing. The most blessed ministries in any arena are also the most criticized. I take great comfort knowing that Greater Shiloh is in good company.

4. *Emergence of new leaders.* After Nehemiah built the wall, new leaders stepped forward. If you wait until you have adequate leadership for the task, you will never complete the vision. If you get on the task God has for you, He will supply the leaders—because God resources what He plans. If you build it … they will come. If you build vision, God will send the leaders you need to accomplish that vision. God often parts the waters only after we step away from the safety of the shore into the river of vision.

I am continually amazed at the quality of people, especially new leaders, God has sent to this church. I am equally taken by the leaders in hiding, folk who were already here, that God has inspired to assume leadership roles.

5. *Major contributions by the people.* The impressive thing is that it shows that when vision catches on, people will contribute. The same people who in Nehemiah 5 complained that they did not have food to eat or money to pay their taxes were then giving in record-setting ways. People will give to vision above anything else. Churches do not have financial problems, they have vision problems. When the vision is clearly defined and people are fully on board, giving is not a problem. People will give to needs only if/when the needs are well-expressed. When they understand the need, most people will respond. People will give to a budget rarely, if at all. No one is motivated to meet the church budget when his or her own budget is in trouble. People give to vision. As they learn the vision, they will give to the vision.

Greater Shiloh has proven this principle to be true. In 2003, 281 people, largely widows, elderly, and many from regular blue-collar jobs, pledged to give 1.3 million dollars over a three-year period because they were inspired about the visionary future of our church. Today, the annual income has consistently exceeded $1.5 million in each of the past four years, during one of the worst recession periods in America, because people are inspired by the vision they see going forth.

6. *Renewed commitment to worship and obedience.* Nehemiah chapters 8, 9, and 10 describe the renewal of the people that results from their commitment to God's vision. This renewed commitment is seen in three ways. Chapter 8 tells us that they read the book of the law together. In chapter 9, the people practiced public confession. There is such a spirit of renewal taking place that after they read the Scripture for hours, they stayed even longer to confess their sins publicly and to worship. They also made a covenant with God. They were so serious about their commitment that they put it in writing. Chapter 10 gives us the list of all the leaders of the people who signed this covenant with God.

Vision produces a new commitment. Program-driven churches tend to become shallow because they get easily sidetracked into tradition and legalism. Any time a program or method becomes the unchallenged standard, the drift in effectiveness is inevitably downward. When methods become sacred, they are rarely, if ever, truly evaluated. They become ecclesiastical ruts. This is the trap of tradition. It can cause us to confuse the sacred message with the temporal method. Soon we forget that it is the content of the Gospel that is sacred, not the container in which it is delivered.

It must be said that tradition is not a bad word. A tradition is a one-time creative method that worked so well that it became the standard method of operation. Any church that makes its programs, traditions, and methods into standards which cannot be challenged, evaluated, or replaced runs the risk of falling into legalism. While legalism may look like the real thing, it is actually one of the shallowest expressions of Christianity in the world today.

When God changes a church, a new method is often given. For us, it was the purpose-driven model of ministry. Purpose-driven churches tend to be more balanced because they discover and implement God's plan for the church. They often escape the shallowness that can occur in churches that are totally seeker-driven. They also avoid the trap of tradition and legalism that often accompanies being program-driven. If the purpose-driven church continues to reinvent and redefine itself by the constant pursuit of God and His vision for the church, balance is the result. Far from being shallow, such churches are, in fact, moving quickly toward being biblically functioning communities. When vision is fully pursued, the results are a renewed commitment to the Bible, to confession and repentance, and to a covenant-oriented relationship to God.

7. *New people join.* Chapters 11 and 12 document the vast numbers of people who moved into the newly walled city of Jerusalem. In Nehemiah 11:1, there was such excitement about the new vision that they held a lottery to determine who could move into the city. Wouldn't it be nice if we had such huge crowds wanting to get in that we had to hold a lottery in order to decide who could come to church? Vision always attracts other people. That is because people are drawn to churches that are passionate about what they are doing and that know where they are going.

People will flock to churches where God is obviously at work. In the short period of time that we have been operating in our new facility, more than 2,000 new people have united in fellowship with us, most of whom were new converts.

8. *Openness to further change.* Chapter 13 says, "And Nehemiah introduced many other changes and reforms." A completed vision leads to openness to further change. Why? Because a proven track record is obvious and evident, and a proven track record leads to trust.

We have been able to implement a series of changes within the church and expansion of the facility is taking place as I write this new edition. Our credibility among community leaders has grown and ministry presence has become more noted with greater influence yet to follow, because we have established a proven record of success.

Cutting-edge churches are always in a change mode. Change is a normal part of healthy living. Every living organism goes through change. Change is a normal part of church life. Every growing church goes through change. Purpose-driven churches are no longer afraid of change. They have shifted the focus from *can we make this transition?* to *which transition do we need to make next?*

When vision has caught on in a church, the evidence is clearly visible. The transitions are being completed with an obvious demonstration that

God is at work. Although there is continued opposition and criticism, there are also new leaders emerging. The people of the church are contributing to the work and growing in their commitment to worship obedience. There are new people coming to the church, being drawn by the vision of what God is doing there, and there is a growing openness to further change.[66]

Give God all the credit and all the glory for what has taken place. Nothing shuts down the work of God in His church like our taking credit for what He has done. Godliness and arrogance cannot coexist in the same church. Personally, I am so grateful for all of the things that God has done. Know that I speak the sentiment of all of the members of Greater Shiloh. It is so obvious that we would be foolish to accept any form of credit for what we know God has done, is doing, and what we know He is going to do for our ministry.

PART V

We've Only Just Begun

Future Projections for Greater Shiloh

What a wonderful and exciting experience it is to witness the supernatural operations of God in a truly natural and ordinary way. What has happened at Greater Shiloh in the past inspires hope and confidence for the future.

Greater Shiloh Missionary Baptist Church's future is extremely bright. We will continue to make transitions and grow. The growth is going to be phenomenal. Here are some assumptions, projected goals, and transitions that are to be made to foster that phenomenal growth.

Core Ministry—Strong biblical preaching and clear biblical teaching will remain at the center of our ministry, as this is what leads people to faith in Christ.

Approach—We will continue to be purpose-driven; however, we will continually refine our approach and make adjustments as needed.

Target—We will refine the local target audience of the un-churched even more. This year and the years to come we will focus on building and developing a college ministry to target young adults between the ages of 19 and 25. There are several major colleges and universities within our city that we have not reached. When spiritual relations are formed with college-aged students, they develop a bond with that church and will likely continue that relationship as members beyond college. It is a tremendous untapped area for growing people in their faith.

Another group that has been on our radar screen to target includes un-churched men within our community between the ages of 25 and 45. Statistics show that when a woman comes to faith in Christ, 19 percent of the time, her family will follow her. However, when a man comes to faith in Christ, 97 percent of the time his family will follow them.

We have the city of Birmingham, along with the counties of Jefferson, Shelby, and Blount, to draw upon. Those areas provide a vast sea of humanity from which to fish. We are no longer just an African-American church—we have already become multicultural. We do expect to reach people internationally, by providing print materials, including books and Bible study series that include video-based materials.

We will continue to provide devotional messages in print and online. We expect to further utilize major network radio and television processes and all forms of media with more precision. We also will take advantage of all of the available and future social-media platforms such as Facebook, Instagram, and Twitter, as they become available to communicate the message of Christ in contemporary contexts.

This year we will build our own television studio and seek FCC licensing. We will use live streaming more effectively and expand blogging opportunities. We intend to expand our television and radio ministries to reach global audiences. Each of these missionary activities has been designed to help reach targeted audiences.

Schedule—We will add more weekend services as the growth takes place. We will soon expand our midweek worship service, currently taking place only on the fist Wednesdays of each month, to every Wednesday. We will continue to refine our children's church and worship service concurrently being held on Sunday mornings. Regarding our youth, we have experimented with Saturday services during summer months called June Saturday Series, aimed largely at youth. However, we will revisit a growing need to develop a regularly scheduled worship service designed specifically for youth. There are plans to develop a small worship venue just for senior citizens that will incorporate the old hymns and utilize the skills of retired clergy.

Pastor—We will transition away from the senior pastor model currently in place, to one where associate pastors take on larger roles. Our organizational structure has been modified to accommodate this model. We are using volunteer lay directors to lead each of the five teams (Missions, Maturity, Ministry, Membership, and Music Magnification Teams). Each team is assigned a biblical purpose and a target audience of the church as defined in our vision statement. Also, there are sub-teams that fall under each. Our transition will be to ordain and hire pastors instead of lay leaders who can shepherd these teams.

As our church has grown larger, a new level of sensitivity has crept in. This will be true as churches grow larger. The pastor's role has to be redefined so that everyone is clear and understands what to expect. Pastors have to decide which traditional ministry functions he will release for someone else to assume. Also he has to make sure that there is someone willing to assume what he releases and then there is the whole notion of the congregation accepting the change in the pastor's function.

One example in our church is that older members still have a hard time understanding why the pastor does not visit them when they are sick. I still do; however, the primary visitation function has been released to deacons and to designated ordained associate ministers. They help ensure that no one is missed or neglected in receiving Communion. However, people still want to see their pastor. It is understood but must be handled with grace.

My new role in a large growing church has been redefined as being the person who creates, casts, and communicates the vision for the church; the person who connects the church to greater kingdom activities; and the preacher on Sunday mornings. Many other pastoral functions have been released to others who now assume them; and we continue to help the congregation adjust to some of the changing functions delegated to others.

Small Groups—We are currently using the Sunday school model primarily for group study. However, we believe that the church must grow larger and smaller at the same time. As we continue to grow larger numerically, we must develop small groups in order to grow relationally at the same time. I envision that we will expand and transition to affinity small groups as the main source of delivering curriculum, connecting members to one another, and providing caring support for one another. This will cause people to live in community with one another. We will become a church not *with* small groups, but a church *of* small groups. This transition will be ongoing because it has now become impossible for everyone to know everyone.

When we were a small congregation with several hundred members it was quite easy for everyone to know each other. Today we have multiple services and basically two or three different congregations: one congregation that worships at the 8:00 a.m. service; another that worships at the 10:45 service; and then those who have their particular Sundays such as those who come on the first Sunday or the third Sunday or any combination such as that.

Community Development—We have launched two 501(c)(3) community development nonprofit organizations as tools to start revitalization projects in the neighborhood. We expect to equip and empower community residents with tools and opportunities, to help address some of their concerns. We want to inspire people to take charge of their own economic, relational, and spiritual situations. We will reach deeper into the community to impact and address the systems that have kept people from advancing. We will develop partnerships with other churches, community agencies, and various entities to accomplish the task. In addition, we will seek multiple funding sources for ministry activities, initiatives, and community revitalization building projects. We will focus on such issues as economic development, educational intervention, literacy support, job readiness, crime prevention, and the huge issue of health and wellness.

New Facilities—Construction of phase one has recently been completed. We have a beautiful 37,000 square foot worship, educational, and recreational facility. The Greater Shiloh Missionary Baptist Church relocation project is a part of a larger project under way in the area. Our church project will be part of a $40 to $50 million community redevelopment project. The redevelopment segment involves two other churches and an independent developer. The overall redevelopment piece will include the construction of 150 affordable single family homes. The Black Warrior-Cahaba Land Trust Company and Faith Apostolic Church have joined together to develop a park, in a joint public-private investment. The park will represent a unique amenity in urban living; it will have a softball field, tennis courts, walking and bike trails, a soccer field, outdoor basketball courts, and picnic tables. There is a strong belief that timing is everything. We believe that building our vision and carrying out our mission at this time are truly of God.

Phase two of our construction began January 2015. We will expand to provide 540 additional seats in the sanctuary via balcony and gallery; we will add a youth wing to the educational facility, to provide nine additional classrooms, offices, and storage space. We will double the size and capacity of our chapel, which is designed for multipurpose use, including choir rehearsals and children's church. We will convert the old choir room into a modern television studio with three sets for broadcasting church news, community events, and special programming. We will also increase paved parking spaces along with curbs, gutters, and additional sidewalks.

The third phase will focus more on community enhancements. New construction on our property will include a 77,000-square-foot community civic center. The center will include a memorabilia gallery, with computerized kiosks displaying the stories of persons from the West End community who have made significant contributions to society. There will be a college regulation-sized gymnasium, with a large theatrical stage, and fly over for community events including theatrical productions and concerts. The center will also include two racket ball courts, men's and women's locker rooms, a game room, and a swimming pool.

There is a desire to put a medical clinic on-site to serve the community, with comprehensive health and wellness programs. Finally, additional property acquisition will be required to develop a young entrepreneurs' business development center, a place for teaching trades, career skills, business enterprising techniques, and job readiness. The center would serve as a base station for community outreach ministries.

With the continued guidance of God, a strategic focus, a love for lost people, and a willingness to empower others to carry out the work of ministry, I do believe we will maintain that missionary zeal. We have gained momentum; we must now harness it, and allow it to power us through the next few years. For the past five years, we have been very intentional in establishing and creating a culture of excellence in everything that we do. We have fully implemented our own Methods and Procedures for Service (MAPS). When followed this process ensures uniformity of practice and excellence in service. "The LORD hath done great things for us; whereof we are glad" (Psalm 126:3). There is definitely a spirit of excellence in this place.

To ride the momentum of excitement is important for us. We must move even more aggressively forward. "But as it is written, Eye have not seen, nor ear heard, neither have entered into the heart of man, the things which God hath prepared for them that love him" (1 Corinthians 2:9).

CONCLUSION

In thirty-two years of preaching the precious Gospel of our Lord and Savior Jesus Christ and serving one church for the past twenty-nine years, I have learned a lot about God, myself, others, and especially life within the Christian church. My wife and I have grown and learned to create balance in our personal lives, to help us manage ministerial stress. This balance prevents us from becoming burned out in our efforts to serve God through this church.

The information that I have shared here is not based on guesswork; these are the tried-and-true methods and experiences gained by daring to believe God. The entire research and transition project began early in my pastorate and continued more formally with documented research from January 2000 until the present. This process has stretched this pastor to new heights. Through the doctoral course work completed at Louisiana Baptist University (LBU) and the applied studies taken through Asbury Theological Seminary's Beeson Institute for Advanced Church Leadership, this pastor has learned and grown immensely. LBU has provided a rich and lasting theological base derived from intense ministry course work. Sound doctrine has been combined with practical exposure to provide the better of two worlds. The guidance, professional friendships, and relationships established on this journey will last a lifetime.

One of the unique experiences that led to the expansion toward personal transition was participating in the Beeson Institute at Asbury. I had the privilege of traveling to nine cutting-edge churches across America. During each visit, I was blessed to observe a particular practice unique for that church, hear modern church philosophy, talk with volunteers and staff, and see a vast array of facilities. These things have provoked an accelerated knowledge base and a greater understanding of the function of a senior pastor as a visionary leader and a leader of leaders. This has directly increased my effectiveness in my role as senior pastor of Greater Shiloh. This pastor and people have truly developed deeper hearts for God and for the work of ministry to lost people, by becoming a church for un-churched people. I truly understand what it is to be a Great Commission church, on mission in the world for God. I also have acquired a theology for inner-city ministry.

I trust that if you are serious about being on mission for God in this world and serving a church that is on fire for God you must be able to hear and see what God has said and what He is doing and wants to do in you.

Each day, God speaks to us. Sometimes, He invites us to draw close and listen as He reveals Himself, His character, and His direction. Other times He calls us to participate in His purposes. Still other times He simply whispers to remind us of His amazing love for us. There is no magic formula for being able to discern God's voice. We can learn to recognize it the way we recognize the voices of those close to us by knowing Him. And when we know God we can tell if what we are feeling led to do is from Him or not.

It is my belief that vision is seeing what I don't hear—visualizing something before it is. Researcher George Barna says, "Vision for ministry is a clear mental image of a preferable future imparted by God to His chosen servants and is based upon an accurate understanding of God, self, and circumstances."[67]

If our vision comes from God, we will also have a passion for it. In fact, passion fuels vision. If we don't have the emotional fire and heartfelt enthusiasm known as passion, we won't have true vision. Passion shows itself in different ways in different people. In every great, cutting-edge church, this common thread is found: a passion to reach the lost for Christ. If you don't have passion to share the Gospel with those who need it, you won't have vision that matches God's heart.

To test a passion or a vision to see if it is from God, ask these questions:

Would this be a great thing for God?

Would it help hurting people?

Would it bring the best out in me?

Is it something God has given me to do?

I can honestly say yes to each of the above questions as I have looked at the changes and the transitions that have taken place during the long and storied history of this church. I can testify that God has directed the changes and transitions the last fifteen years in this church. I am convinced and very confident that these same kinds and similar results can take place in any church if the principles that have been outlined are followed. Of course it is God, not methods or processes, that ultimately blesses the work.

So before God can do any real redemptive work in the church, He must first do it in the man or woman He has called to lead that particular church. Then God must do a work within the hearts of the people of a particular congregation of people. He must educate them in understanding what He is doing and wants to do. He has already extended an invitation for the church to join Him where He is already at work. But that's what the pastor must see. It is in the Great Commission. Since Jesus spoke those words, He has not withdrawn them; so they become the marching orders for the church. Churches will not change just because we are sick and tired of being sick and tired. Churches will not change because of tradition, intellect, or experience. They will change when God's man catches the biblical vision and begins to teach people the Word of God and to understand and implement strategic processes.

Finally, the pastor must be wise and diligent. He must be wise to understand the dynamics of change and transition. Churches will change—not like turning a small vehicle like a Volkswagen, but more like turning a large vessel like a big ocean liner. It will change, but 10 degrees at a time. Therefore, the pastor must be diligent and stay committed—enduring until the process is complete and the vision has been realized.

Here are some general tips you can use to help further evaluate your church.

- Do a few things well. Create a movement through word-of-mouth.

- Build connections in culture with an eye that sees how people are thinking about church and God and meeting them on their ground.

- Focus on slow and steady growth—making small changes every week and allowing God to produce the tipping point, which may not come in numbers and statistics, but more of an organic movement with stories and relationships.

- Use repetition to create memory markers. Jesus may have preached the same sermons, numerous times, for a reason.

- Focus on the movement over statistics. Looking for unique ways to disperse the Gospel should be more important than trying to fill every seat in the church. This may seem subtle but people can see this a mile away; having integrity in our motives is crucial.

- Study and look at the history of your church in your community. Make an evaluation of the underlying philosophy both from inside the church and out. Don't be afraid to ask someone in the community what they think about your church—and take it seriously.

- Make every effort to care for people over programs; there is perhaps no better way to create an epidemic than the simple art of caring.

- Understand that the movement may be underground—below the radar—but that's how epidemics really begin, with a select and passionate few who influence others who influence others who influence others.

- Of course focus on following Christ in the small and big details of living and being the church.

God truly has changed me, and He has unquestionably changed Greater Shiloh Missionary Baptist Church. I strongly suspect that God wants to change you as well. My personal encouragement to each reader is this: "And let us not be weary in well doing: for in due season we shall reap, if we faint not" (Galatians 6:9). Paul also wrote in Ephesians 3:20-21, "Now unto Him that is able to do exceeding abundantly above all that we ask or think, according to the power that worketh in us, unto Him be glory in the church by Christ Jesus throughout all ages, world without end. Amen."

APPENDIX I

GROWTH STRATEGIES MAP CHURCH YEAR 2000
(Used to Guide the Strategic Process Listed in Part III)

Growth Strategies Map

I	II			III	IV
STRATEGIC VIEW	Church Function Development	Ministry Resources Analysis	Expected Changes/ Results	Actions	Statements Used For Measurement
• Kingdom Principles				Biblical Process Model	
•Great Commission		1.Man hours	1 Hard Changes		- Weekly
•Purpose Statement		2. Space	- Numerical		- Monthly
•Vision Statement		3.People	- Ministries		- Quarterly
•	Five Essential Church Functions	4.Training	- Missions		- Yearly
Discovery of Membership Spiritual Gifts	Evangelism				
Leadership Spiritual Gifts	Discipleship		2 Soft Changes	Programs	
Church Giftedness Composite	Ministry		- Spiritual	Calendars based on priorities	
Community Survey	Fellowship Worship		- Feelings - Moods		
SWOTS	Attitudes Possibility Grids		-	Budgeting based on priorities	

119

NOTES

1. Gerhard Kittel and Gerhard Friedrich, eds., *Theological Dictionary of the New Testament*, translated and abridged by Geoffrey W. Bromiley (Grand Rapids: Eerdmans, 1985), 903.

2. Bill Hull, *The Disciple Making Pastor: The Key to Building Healthy Christians in Today's Church*, with a foreword by Robert E. Coleman (Old Tappan, NJ: Fleming H. Revell, 1988), 89.

3. John A. Broadus, *On the Preparation and Delivery of Sermons*, new and revised edition by Weatherspoon (Nashville: Broadman Press, 1944), 3.

4. Trent C. Butler, ed., *Holman Bible Dictionary* (Nashville: Holman Bible Publishers, 1991), 1132–1133.

5. J. I. Packer, "Authority in Preaching," in *The Gospel in the Modern World*, eds. Martyn Eden and David F. Wells (London: InterVarsity Press, 1991), 199.

6. George Barna, *Leaders on Leadership* (Ventura, CA: Regal Books, 1997), 18–25.

7. Ibid., 18.

8. Ibid.

9. Kittel and Friedrich, *Theological Dictionary of the New Testament*, 562.

10. Henry Chadwick, ed., *The Pelican History of the Church*, vol. 6; and *A History of Christian Missions*, by Stephen Neill (New York: Penguin Books, 1964; reprint 1982), 23.

11. Trent C. Butler, ed., *Holman Bible Dictionary*, "Church" by Harold S. Songer (Nashville: Holman Bible Publishers, 1991), 259.

12. Ibid.

13. Rick Warren, *The Purpose Driven Church* (Grand Rapids: Zondervan, 1995), 81.

14. Leith Anderson, *A Church for the 21st Century* (Minneapolis: Bethany House, 1992), 130.

15. Ibid., 129.

16. Robert C. Linthicum, *City of God City of Satan* (Grand Rapids: Zondervan, 1991), 23.

17. Ibid., 262.

18. Ibid., 263–266.

19. William Bridges, *Managing Transitions: Making the Most of Change*, 2nd edition (Cambridge, MA: Perseus Publishing, 2003), 3.

20. Craig A. Satterlee, *When God Speaks through Change: Preaching in Times of Congregational Transition* (Herndon, VA: The Alban Institute, 2005), 3.

21. Ibid., 4.

22. Joseph R. Jeter Jr., *Crisis Preaching: Personal and Public* (Nashville: Abingdon Press, 1998), 13.

23. Ibid., 14.

24. Satterlee, *When God Speaks through Change*, 6–7.

25. Bridges, *Managing Transitions*, 39–56.

26. Satterlee, *When God Speaks through Change*, 8.

27. Ibid.

28. Ibid., 9.

29. Ibid., 10.

30. Fred B. Craddock, *Preaching* (Nashville: Abingdon Press, 1985), 201.

31. Walter Brueggemann, *Finally Comes the Poet* (Philadelphia: Fortress, 1989), 79–110.

32. Satterlee, *When God Speaks through Change*, 13.

33. Ronald J. Allen, *Preaching the Topical Sermon* (Louisville: Westminster John Knox, 1992), 21–22.

34. Charles L. Campbell, *The Word Before the Powers: An Ethic of Preaching* (Louisville: Westminster John Knox, 2002), 68–69.

35. William B. Easum, "Turning a Church Around Is a Dangerous Calling" (lecture, Beeson Institute for Advanced Church Leadership, February 2004).

36. Dale E. Galloway, "Taking the Mystery Out of Change," in *New Ideas in Church Vitality* (October 1999), 21–22.

37. Ibid., 22.

38. Ibid.

39. Dale Galloway, "Becoming a Successful Change Agent" (lecture, Beeson Institute for Advanced Church Leadership, February 22, 2004).

40. William B. Easum, "Transition Issues in Spiritual Redwood Churches" (lecture, Beeson Institute for Advanced Church Leadership, February 24, 2005).

41. Ibid., 3.

42. Ibid., 5.

43. Ibid., 6.

44. Ibid., 8.

45. Gene Mims, *Kingdom Principles for Church Growth* (Nashville: Convention Press, 1994), 6.

46. Ibid, 9–11.

47. Gene Mims and Michael Miller, *Kingdom Principles Growth Strategies: Leader's Guide* (Nashville: Convention Press, 1994), 1–72.

48. Ibid., 10.

49. Warren, *The Purpose-Driven Church*, 80.

50. Ibid., 100–101.

51. Aubrey Malphurs, *Advanced Strategic Planning: A New Model for Church and Ministry Leaders* (Grand Rapids: Baker Books, 1999), 105–106.

52. Appendix 1 (Strategic Plan 2000).

53. Appendix 1 (Strategic Plan 2000, Pastor's Ministry Gift composite).

54. Ibid. (Church's Ministry Giftedness composite).

55. Mims and Miller, *Leaders Guide*, 13.

56. Ibid., 61.

57. Appendix 1 (Strategic Plan 2000, Function Grids).

58. Ibid. (Possibility Grids).

59. Ibid. (Hard Changes Chart).

60. Appendix 2 (Church-wide Survey and the results).

61. Appendices 3–7 (Annual Strategic Plan Updates and Evaluations).

62. William J. Abraham, *The Logic of Evangelism* (Grand Rapids: Eerdmans, 1989), 4.

63. Prince E. Burroughs, *The Ministry of the Deacon* (Nashville: Sunday School Publishing Board, 1995), 32.

64. Appendix on Leadership School Modules.

65. Dan Southerland, *Transitioning* (Grand Rapids: Zondervan, 1999), 20.

66. Ibid., 149–165.

67. George Barna, *The Power of Vision: How You Can Capture and Apply God's Vision for Your Ministry* (Ventura, CA: Regal Books, 1992), 28.

BIBLIOGRAPHY

Bible Study Sources

McReynolds, Paul R. *Nestle Aland 26th Edition Greek New Testament with McReynolds English Interlinear*. Oak Harbor, Washington: Logos Research Systems, Inc., 1997.

Vine's Expository Dictionary of New Testament Words. Oliphants, Ltd.,1940. First published in 1940 by Oliphants Ltd. (4 volumes). One Volume, 1952.

Church Mission

Allen, Clifton, J., ed. *The Broadman Commentary*. Vol. 11, *2 Corinthians – Philemon*, by Ralph P. Martin. Nashville, Tennessee: Broadman Press, 1971.

Butler, Trent C., ed. *Holman Bible Dictionary*. Nashville, Tennessee: Holman Bible Publishers, 1991.

Chadwick, Henry, ed. *The Pelican History of the Church*. Vol. 6, *A History of Christian Missions,* by Stephen Neill. New York: Penguin Books, 1964. Reprint 1982.

Conner, W. T. *Christian Doctrine*. Nashville, Tennessee: Broadman Press, 1937.

Crabtree, Davida Foy. *The Empowering Church: How One Congregation Supports Lay People's Ministries in the World*. The Alban Institute, 1989. Reprinted 1996.

Criswell, W. A. *The Doctrine of the Church*. Nashville, Tennessee: Convention Press, 1980. Reprint 1981.

Dockery, David S., ed. *The New American Commentary*. Vol. 22, *Matthew*, by Craig L. Blomberg. Nashville, Tennessee: Broadman Press, 1992.

George, Timothy. *Theology of the Reformers*. Nashville, Tennessee: Broadman Press, 1988.

Hobbs, Herschel H. *The Baptist Faith and Message*. Nashville, Tennessee: Convention Press, 1971. Reprinted 1979, 1980, 1981, 1982, 1983.

Humpreys, Fisher. *Thinking About God: An Introduction to Christian Theology*. New Orleans: Insight Press, 1974.

Kittel, Gerhard, and Gerhard Friedrich, eds. *Theological Dictionary of the New Testament*. Translated and abridged by Geoffrey W. Bromiley. Grand Rapids, Michigan: William B. Eerdmans Publishing Company, 1985.

Kung, Hans. *The Church*. New York: Burns and Oates Ltd., 1967. Reprint, Garden City, New York: Image Books, 1976.

Leonard, Bill J. *The Nature of the Church*. Layman's Library of Christian Doctrine. Nashville, Tennessee: Broadman Press, 1986.

Moltmann, Jurgen. *The Church in the Power of the Spirit: A Contribution to Messianic Ecclesiology*. Translated by Margaret Kohl. New York: Harper and Row Publishers, 1977.

Moody, Dale. *The Word of Truth: A Summary of Christian Doctrine Based on Biblical Revelation*. Grand Rapids, Michigan: William B. Eerdmans Publishing Company, 1981.

Orr, Robert A. *Being God's People: A Southern Baptist Church on Bold Mission*. Nashville, Tennessee: Convention Press, 1987: Reprint 1989.

Congregational Studies and Research

Anderson, Leith. *A Church for the 21st Century*. Minneapolis, Minnesota: Bethany House Publishers, 1992.

Babbie, Earl R. *The Practice of Social Research,* 7th ed. Belmont, California: Wadsworth Publishing Company, 1995.

Bakke, Raymond J., and Samuel K. Roberts. *The Expanded Mission of 'Old First' Churches.* Valley Forge, Pennsylvania: Judson Press, 1986.

Barna, George. *User Friendly Churches: What Christians Need to Know About the Churches People Love to Go To.* Ventura, California: Regal Books, 1991.

Callahan, Kennon L. *Twelve Keys to an Effective Church: Strategic Planning for Mission.* San Francisco: Harper, 1983.

Carroll, W. Jackson, Carl S. Dudley, and William McKinney, eds. *Handbook for Congregational Studies.* Nashville, Tennessee: Abingdon Press, 1987.

Dale, Robert D. *To Dream Again.* Nashville, Tennessee: Broadman Press, 1981.

Drummond, Lewis A. *The Awakening that Must Come.* Nashville, Tennessee: Broadman Press, 1978.

Hunter, George G., III. *How to Reach Secular People.* Nashville, Tennessee: Abingdon Press, 1992.

Martin, Glen, and Gary McIntosh. *The Issachar Factor: Understanding Trends that Confront Your Church and Designing a Strategy for Success.* Nashville, Tennessee: Broadman and Holman Publishers, 1993.

McGavran, Donald and George G. Hunter III. *Church Growth: Strategies that Work, Creative Leadership Series,* ed. Lyle E. Schaller. Nashville, Tennessee: Abingdon Press, 1986. Seventh printing, 1986.

Mead, Loren B. *The Once and Future Church: Reinventing the Congregation for a New Mission Frontier.* n. p.: The Alban Institute, 1991. Reprint, 1992 and 1993.

Myers, William R. *Research in Ministry: A Primer for the Doctor of Ministry Program.* With an introduction by W. Widick Schroeder. Chicago: Exploration Press, 1993.

Neighbour, Ralph. *The Seven Last Words of the Church.* Foreword by Leighton Ford. Grand Rapids, Michigan: Zondervan Publishing House, 1973. Second printing, 1973.

Pappas, Anthony, and Scott Planting. *Mission: The Small Church Reaches Out.* Valley Forge, Pennsylvania: Judson Press, 1993.

Patten, Mildred L. *Understanding Research Methods.* Los Angeles: Pyrezak Publishing, 1997.

Powell, Paul W. *Building an Evangelistic Church.* Dallas, Texas: Annuity Board of the Southern Baptist Convention, 1991.

Rainer, Thom S. *Eating the Elephant: Bite-sized Steps to Achieve Long-term Growth in Your Church.* Nashville, Tennessee: Broadman and Holman Publishers, 1994.

Robinson, Darrell W. *Total Church Life: Exalt, Equip, Evangelize.* Nashville, Tennessee: Broadman Press, 1985. Revised and expanded edition, 1993.

Rowatt, G. Wade, Jr. "What is Pastoral Research?" *Review and Expositor* 79 (Summer 1982): 503-11.

Russell, Keith A. *In Search of the Church: New Testament Images for Tomorrow's Congregations.* The Alban Institute, 1994.

Schaller, Lyle E. *44 Steps Up Off the Plateau.* Nashville, Tennessee: Abingdon Press, 1993.

Tennessee Baptist Convention. *The Tennessee Baptist Convention Journal.* Brentwood, Tennessee: Program Services Division, 1991–1996.

Van Engen, Charles. *God's Missionary People: Rethinking the Purpose of the Local Church.* Foreword by Arthur F. Glasser. Grand Rapids, Michigan: Baker Book House, 1991.

Wagner, C. Peter. *Churches that Pray: How Prayer Can Help Revitalize Your Congregation and Break Down the Walls Between Your Church and Your Community.* Ventura, California: Regal Books, 1993.

Warren, Rick. *The Purpose-Driven Church.* Grand Rapids, Michigan: Zondervan Publishing Company, 1995.

White, James Emery. *Opening the Front Door: Worship and Church Growth.* Foreword by Rick Warren. Nashville, Tennessee: Convention Press, 1992.

Educational

Angelo, Thomas A., and K. Patricia Cross. *Classroom Assessment Techniques: A Handbook for College Teachers.* San Francisco, California: Jossey-Bass Publishers, 1993.

Evangelism

Bailey, Waylon. *As You Go: Biblical Foundations for Evangelism.* New Orleans, Louisiana: Insight Press, 1981.

Bisagno, John R. *How to Build an Evangelistic Church.* Nashville, Tennessee: Broadman Press, 1971.

Clemons, William P. *Discovering the Depths.* Nashville, Tennessee: Broadman Press, 1976.

Coleman, Robert E. *The Master Plan of Evangelism.* New Jersey: Fleming H. Revell Company, 1963.

Drummond, Lewis A. *Leading Your Church in Evangelism.* Nashville, Tennessee: Broadman Press, 1975.

Eims, Leroy. *Winning Ways: The Adventure of Sharing Christ*. Wheaton, Illinois: Victor Books, 1975.

Hogue, C. B. *Love Leaves No Choice: Life-Style Evangelism*. Waco, Texas: Word Books Publishers, 1976.

Kuiper, R. B. *God-Centered Evangelism: A Presentation of the Scriptural Theology of Evangelism*. Carlisle, Pennsylvania: The Banner of Truth Trust, 1961.

McIntosh, Duncan. *The Everyday Evangelist*. Valley Forge, Pennsylvania: Judson Press, 1984.

Miles, Delos. *How Jesus Won Persons*. Nashville, Tennessee: Broadman Press, 1982.

Robinson, Darrell W. *People Sharing Jesus*. Nashville, Tennessee: Thomas Nelson Publishers, 1995.

Salter, Darius. *American Evangelism: Its Theology and Practice*. Grand Rapids, Michigan: Baker Books, 1996.

Stott, John R. W. *Our Guilty Silence*. Grand Rapids, Michigan: William B. Eerdmans Publishing Company, 1982.

Sweazey, George Edgar. *Effective Evangelism: The Greatest Work in the World*. New York: Harper & Brothers Publishers, 1953.

Welch, Bobby H. *Evangelism Through the Sunday School: A Journey of Faith*. Nashville, Tennessee: Lifeway Press, 1997.

Pastoral

Bryson, Harold T., and James C. Taylor. *Building Sermons to Meet People's Needs*. Nashville, Tennessee: Broadman Press, 1980.

Brister, C. W. *Pastoral Care in the Church.* New York: Harper & Row Publishers, 1977.

Cothen, Joe H. *Equipped for Good Work,* Gretna, Louisiana: Pelican Publishing Company, 1987.

Crabtree, T. T. *The Zondervan Pastor's Annual.* Grand Rapids, Michigan: Zondervan Publishing House, 2000.

Schaller, Lyle E. *The Change Agent: The Strategy of Innovative Leadership.* Nashville, Tennessee: Abingdon Press, 1972.

Preaching and Leadership

Adams, Jay Edward. *Preaching with Purpose: A Comprehensive Textbook on Biblical Preaching.* Grand Rapids, Michigan: Presbyterian and Reformed Publishing Company, 1982.

Barry, James C. *Preaching in Today's World.* Nashville, Tennessee: Broadman Press, 1984.

Bohen, Rudolf. *Preaching and Community.* Richmond, Virginia: John Knox Press, 1965.

Broadus, John A. *On the Preparation and Delivery of Sermons.* New and Revised Edition, Revised by Jesse Burton Weatherspoon. Nashville, Tennessee: Broadman Press, 1944.

Callahan, Kennon L. *Effective Church Leadership: Building on the Twelve Keys.* San Francisco: Harper & Row, Publishers, 1990.

Craddock, Fred B. *Preaching.* Nashville, Tennessee: Abingdon Press, 1985.

Daane, James. *Preaching with Confidence: A Theological Essay on the Power of the Pulpit.* Grand Rapids, Michigan: William B. Eerdmans Publishing Company, 1980.

Duduit, Michael, ed. *Handbook of Contemporary Preaching.* Nashville, Tennessee: Broadman Press, 1992.

Hamilton, Donald L. *Homiletical Handbook.* Nashville, Tennessee: Broadman Press, 1992.

Henrichsen, Walter A. *Disciples Are Made Not Born.* Wheaton, Illinois: Victor Books, 1988.

Hesselbein, Frances, Marshall Goldsmith, and Richard Beckhard, eds. *The Leader of the Future: New Visions, Strategies, and Practices for the Next Era.* Foreword by Peter F. Drucker. San Francisco: Jossey-Bass Publishers, 1996.

Hull, Bill. *The Disciple Making Pastor: The Key to Building Healthy Christians in Today's Church.* Foreword by Robert E. Coleman. Old Tappan, New Jersey: Fleming H. Revell, 1988.

Hull, William E. Unpublished manuscript on strategic preaching, 1998. TMs (photocopy). Author's personal manuscript. Birmingham, Alabama.

Johnson, Laney L. *The Church: God's People on Mission.* Nashville, Tennessee: Convention Press, 1995.

Killinger, John. *The Centrality of Preaching in the Total Task of Ministry.* Waco, Texas: Wood Books, Publisher, 1969.

McClure, John S. *The Roundtable Pulpit: Where Leadership and Preaching Meet.* Nashville, Tennessee: Abingdon Press, 1995.

Means, James E. *Effective Pastors for a New Century: Helping Leaders Strategize for Success.* Foreword by Bill Hull. Grand Rapids, Michigan: Baker Books, 1993.

Miller, Calvin. *The Empowered Communicator: 7 Keys to Unlocking an Audience.* Nashville, Tennessee: Broadman and Holman Publishers, 1994.

Packer, J. I. "Authority in Preaching," in *The Gospel in the Modern World*, ed. Martyn Eden and David F. Wells. London: InterVarsity Press, 1991.

Powell, Paul W. *The Church Today*. Nashville, Tennessee: Annuity Board of the Southern Baptist Convention, 1997.

Stevens, R. Paul, and Phil Collins. *The Equipping Pastor: A Systems Approach to Congregational Leadership*. The Alban Institute, 1993.

Stott, John R. W. *Between Two Worlds: The Art of Preaching in the Twentieth Century*. Grand Rapids, Michigan: William B. Eerdmans Publishing Company, 1982.

Swindoll, Charles R. *Living Above the Level of Mediocrity: A Commitment to Excellence*. Dallas, Texas: World Publishing, 1989.

Theology

Conner, W. C. *Christian Doctrine*. Nashville, Tennessee: Broadman Press, 1937.

Dallas Theological Seminary Thesis Style Committee. "Supplement to Kate L. Turabian, A Manual for Writers of Terms Papers, Theses, and Dissertations, 6th ed." Dallas: Dallas Theological Seminary, 1999.

Erickson, Mildred J. *Christian Theology*. Grand Rapids, Michigan: Baker Book House, 1985.

George, Timothy. *Theology of the Reformers*. Nashville, Tennessee: Broadman Press, 1988.

Grenz, Stanley J. *Theology for the Community of God*. Nashville, Tennessee: Broadman and Holman Publishers, 1994.

Humphreys, Fisher. *Thinking About God*. New Orleans, Louisiana: Insight Press, 1974.

Ladd, George Eldon. *A Theology of the New Testament.* Grand Rapids, Michigan: William B. Eerdmans Publishing Company, 1974.

McGrath, Alister E. *Christian Theology, An Introduction, 2nd Edition.* Cambridge, Massachusetts: Blackwell Publishers, 1997.

Stagg, Frank. *New Testament Theology.* Nashville, Tennessee: Broadman Press, 1962.

Strunk, William, Jr., and E. B. White. *The Elements of Style,* 4th ed. Boston: Allyn and Bacon, 1999.

Turabian, Kate L. *A Manual for Writers of Term Papers, Theses and Dissertations.* Revised by John Grossman and Alice Bennett, 6th ed. Chicago: University of Chicago Press, 1996.

Vyhmeister, Nancy Jean. *Quality Research Papers: For Students of Religion and Theology.* Grand Rapids: Zondervan Publishing House, 2001.

Biographical Sketch of
Dr. Michael W. Wesley Sr.

D r. Michael W. Wesley Sr. is a native of Birmingham, Alabama, where he was educated in the public schools. He graduated from Tennessee State University, Nashville, Tennessee, with a Bachelor of Science degree in Music Education. He received a Master's degree in Music Education; a Class A certification in School Principalship; and the Educational Specialist degree in Educational Leadership from Samford University in Birmingham, Alabama. In addition, Wesley received a Bible Diploma and Bible Certification from Birmingham Baptist Bible College. He earned the Doctor of Ministry degree at Louisiana Baptist University and Theological Seminary in Shreveport, Louisiana.

Wesley has enjoyed a balanced educational and religious life. As a product of the racially segregated South, he was educated during the period when the door of integration first opened. He was among the first to make the transition by attending both all-black and then all-white schools. The multicultural exposure has helped shape his understanding of the world and the social struggles that humans have in trying to live out Christian values.

Wesley retired in 2003 after a brilliant twenty-six-year career as an educator in the Birmingham Public Schools. He served as a teacher, assistant principal, and principal of three different schools (Powderly Elementary; Arrington Middle; and Woodlawn High School, where he was the first African-American principal). He served on the Central Office staff as Extended Day Principal and Coordinator of Safe and Drug-Free Schools.

Wesley is regularly sought after to speak in both schools and churches. He has had the privilege of speaking across the nation and in several foreign countries. His spiritual gifts of teaching and preaching are well-documented. He is a member of many organizations. His civic and professional associations are too numerous to mention. He has authored two books: *When God Changes a Church* (1st and 2nd Editions) and *Everybody Deserves A Good Funeral.*

Wesley has served God all of his life through the local church. As a youth in his home church, South Elyton Baptist, he taught the intermediate Sunday school class and served as assistant clerk of the church, responsible for recording the contributions of the membership. Later he served as a trustee, an ordained deacon, and a choir director before becoming licensed and ordained into the Gospel ministry.

He has served as the pastor of Greater Shiloh Missionary Baptist Church for twenty-nine years. He has a great love for people and for learning.

He is married to the former Venita Burkes of Columbus, Ohio, and is the father of two sons—Rev. Michael Wesley Jr. and James Edward Wesley. He and his wife are the proud grandparents of three grandchildren: Ethan James, Michaiah Grace, and McKinleigh Reign.

CPSIA information can be obtained
at www.ICGtesting.com
Printed in the USA
BVHW041100230421
605718BV00011B/342